Revolutionary
A Walking Guide Dublin
1912–1923

JOHN GIBNEY, from Dublin, is currently DFAT 100 Project Coordinator with the Royal Irish Academy's Documents on Irish Foreign Policy project. He has lectured at Trinity College Dublin and University College Dublin and has been a research fellow at the University of Notre Dame and NUI Galway. He worked on the Historical Walking Tours of Dublin until 2015 and is the author of *Dublin: An Illustrated History* (2017), *A Short History of Ireland, 1500–2000* (Yale University Press, 2018) and a photographic history of Dublin during the War of Independence and Civil War (2018).

DONAL FALLON, from Dublin, is co-founder of the popular 'Come Here To Me' blog, and has worked as a walking tour guide in the city. His work has appeared in *The Irish Times*, *History Ireland* and other outlets, and he is a frequent contributor to Newstalk radio. He lectures with the Adult Education Department of University College Dublin. His previous publications include a biography of Major John MacBride (2015) and a history of the Nelson Pillar (2014).

Revolutionary
A Walking Guide
Dublin
1912–1923

**John Gibney and
Donal Fallon**

The Collins Press

CONTENTS

ACKNOWLEDGEMENTS

This book has its origins in the authors' background in conducting historical walking tours in Dublin, and they would like to thank a few colleagues and friends who have also walked the beat or otherwise lent a hand over the years: Peter Ballagh, Lorcan Collins, Conor Dodd, Tara Doyle, Mark Duncan, Las Fallon, Liz Gillis, Tommy Graham, Brian Hanley, Carole Holohan, Máire Kennedy, Edward Madigan, Conor McNamara, Ciarán Murray, Grace O'Keefe, Paul Reynolds, and the staff of University College Dublin Adult Education Centre. Finally, we would like to dedicate this book to the memory of the late Shane Kenna and the late Shane Mac Thomáis.

INTRODUCTION

In James Joyce's short story 'Ivy Day in the Committee Room', a group of unenthusiastic canvassers take a break from electioneering for a nationalist candidate in an unspecified room on Wicklow Street. Bottles of porter arrive, and, given that it takes place on 'Ivy Day' (6 October, the anniversary of the death of Charles Stewart Parnell), talk turns wistfully to their lost leader. In this sense, the characters look resolutely backwards to what might have been, in a concrete example of the paralysis that Joyce famously spoke of. Yet within a number of years of the publication in 1914 of *Dubliners*, the city in which it was set was gripped by political and social upheaval far removed from the concerns and beliefs of the characters in the committee room. Joyce's characters were serving a cause – that of Irish Home Rule – that was in the doldrums at the turn of the twentieth century. Yet had the story been set a decade or two later, the cause they served would have been dead, swept away by the revolution that took place in Ireland between 1912 and 1923. What this book is intended to do is to explore that revolution in Ireland's capital, far beyond Joyce's fictional room in Wicklow Street.

DUBLIN ON THE EVE OF REVOLUTION

Dublin in the second decade of the twentieth century was a city of over 300,000 people. Viewed from above, the city was almost oval shaped, being largely confined between the Royal Canal to the north and the Grand Canal to the south, with some urban growth spilling over these boundaries in the shape of new suburbs, especially south of the Grand Canal. Viewed from street level, Dublin was a city that had been shaped in the Georgian and Victorian eras. From the late seventeenth century onwards, a street plan had been created that was still largely the framework of the early twentieth-century city. Private developments and major public building characterised the remarkable growth of the Georgian era, and this was added to in the nineteenth century. Dublin had a distinctive history in the nineteenth century, one that was shaped, as ever, by the wider patterns of Irish history.

The origins of Dublin can be traced back to the Vikings, and by the early modern period it had become a colonial bridgehead for the British conquest and colonisation of that era. It grew dramatically in the eighteenth century as the capital of a semi-autonomous kingdom, governed by a Protestant landowning elite of British descent, and subservient, to all intents and purposes, to Britain. The Act of Union that came into effect in 1801 integrated Ireland into an expanded United Kingdom, and one concrete manifestation of this was the integration of the Irish parliament, previously based in the elaborate Parliament House on College Green, into its British counterpart in London. The loss of the parliament also ensured that Ireland's resident aristocracy slowly vacated the city as they lost a prime reason for being there, and the sense of decline that followed the union was exacerbated by economic downturns after the end of the Napoleonic Wars in 1815, and the ending of customs barriers with Britain in the 1820s. Yet Dublin continued to grow in the nineteenth century, albeit at a reduced rate. It had been a city of administration for centuries, housing the main courts, banking services, government and what was until the nineteenth century Ireland's only university (i.e. Trinity College). Dublin continued to be a major regional capital within the United Kingdom, though its traditional industrial base (such as textile manufacturing) was whittled away. Dublin was the largest port on the island of Ireland and served as a transit point for the export of food and the importation of British goods. The vast bulk of its trade was with Britain, rather than the rest of the world. Crucially, Dublin was not an industrial city; it was distinctive amongst the major cities of what was then the United Kingdom in lacking heavy industry. By 1911, perhaps only 20 per cent of the male workforce was employed in manufacturing.

What Dublin did have by the turn of the twentieth century was a much-improved infrastructure, in the form of railways and an extensive tram network, and a new ring of suburbs around the fringes of the two canals. These were related to a significant social change, as the emerging Catholic and Protestant middle classes of the Victorian era abandoned the inner city. The converse of this was that much of the inner city had, in the second half of the nineteenth century, declined into tenements. In Dublin, a higher ratio of the population lived in slums than in any comparable British city.

In religious terms, Dublin was still approximately 83 per cent Catholic, according to the 1911 census, though migration to the suburbs ensured that in some of these there was a much higher proportion of Protestants, who were often politically unionist. Nationalist Dublin was firmly in the hands of the Home Rule movement, but there was scope for more radical (albeit fringe) political parties, such as Arthur Griffith's Sinn Féin, not to mention the labour and suffrage movements. The city had its own police force, the Dublin Metropolitan Police or DMP, often populated by migrants from the country. Indeed, Dublin had a sizeable immigrant population, largely from neighbouring counties but also from overseas, with the demands for skilled labour and the presence of the British Army ensuring that British immigrants were quite numerous. And sport, leisure, theatrical venues, pubs and consumer culture were also part and parcel of life in a city that was soon to become one of the focal points of the Irish revolution.

THE REVOLUTION

We saw a vision of Ireland, free, pure, happy. We did not realise this vision. But we saw it.

Helena Molony, cited in Fearghal McGarry, The Abbey Rebels of 1916: A Lost Revolution *(Dublin, 2015).*

The area of the city is approximately 8 square miles, and if the suburbs, including Kingstown, are included, the area of Greater Dublin is about 14 square miles. The population of the city is 230,000, and the inclusion of the suburbs adds about 170,000 to the above figure ... the city is divided, roughly speaking, into two equal parts by the river Liffey which is also crossed by numerous bridges. It is a maze of narrow streets and alleys set in no order. There is little definite residential area, slums and tenement houses are found everywhere, and in the older part of the city there are many ramifications of underground cellars in which men, munitions, and munitions factories can be hidden. There are innumerable small shops and comparatively few large stores. It is, in fact, an ideal town for guerilla warfare.

The British military's assessment of Dublin during the War of Independence, from the 'Record of the rebellion in Ireland in 1920–21', cited in William Sheehan, Fighting for Dublin: the British Battle for Dublin, 1919–21 *(Cork, 2007).*

Defining the Irish revolutionary period is in itself a difficult task. When the Bureau of Military History began the task, in the 1940s, of collecting memories of the Irish revolution from those who had participated in it, their official brief noted their task as being 'to assemble and co-ordinate material to form the basis for the compilation of the history of the movement for Independence from the formation of the Irish Volunteers on 25th November 1913, to the 11th July 1921.' Yet even that has its origins in the Home Rule crisis of 1912–14. And what of the Civil War of 1922–23? For our purposes, the revolution took place in the eleven years between 1912 and 1923; this book glances beyond both of these dates, but what follows is a brief outline of the key events that took place between those two dates.

In 1912 the Home Rule nationalists of the Irish Parliamentary Party, led by John Redmond, were the dominant force in nationalist

Ireland, demanding as they did a modest form of devolution for Ireland within the UK: 'Home Rule'. This reflected the aspirations of much of the Irish public themselves (or at least those entitled to vote), who consistently elected the men of the Irish Parliamentary Party to represent them in Westminster. When the Liberal Prime Minister Herbert Asquith visited Dublin in 1912, on the cusp of legislating to establish a Home Rule parliament in Ireland, he was regaled with nationalist ballads such as 'A Nation Once Again' and 'God Save Ireland'.

The promise of Home Rule, however modest, prompted a furious response from Irish unionists, the vast majority of whom were Protestants, and resided in the northern province of Ulster. Yet unionism was not confined to there. Unionists feared that Home Rule would lead to discrimination by the Catholic majority on a number of fronts, and Ulster Unionists mobilised to resist Home Rule under the leadership of figures such as the Dublin-born barrister and MP for Trinity College Dublin, Edward Carson. The creation of the paramilitary Ulster Volunteer Force (UVF), with the express purpose of resisting Home Rule by force, prompted Asquith's government to contemplate partitioning Ireland into separate jurisdictions (a decision that would finally come to pass in 1920). It also prompted Irish nationalists to establish the Irish Volunteers as a counterpart, and the prospect of two private armies fighting each other over the question of Ireland's future was defused only by the outbreak of European war in August 1914.

The Irish revolutionary period can only be understood in its global context, as it was shaped in so many ways by the First World War and its aftermath. Dublin went to war in 1914, and the next two years saw the city wracked by food and fuel shortages, not to mention a mounting casualty toll as men from Dublin enlisted in the British Army to fight. But as an old cliché would have it, England's difficulty was seen as Ireland's opportunity. Separatist republicans, who remained a vibrant minority in Edwardian Ireland, saw an opportunity to launch their own attack on British rule in Ireland.

The Easter Rising of April 1916 was the result, a separatist uprising carried out by seemingly disparate political voices under the broad banner of seeking Irish independence.

The Irish Volunteers brought the greatest body of men to the fight. By the time of the Rising, this movement had split into factions, with the vast majority of members supporting John Redmond's call to enlist and fight in the First World War in order to secure the Home Rule bill promised by the British before the war; the minority who opposed this had kept the name of Irish Volunteers, and went on to fight in the Rising. There was also the Irish Citizen Army, established out of the bitter class confrontation of the 1913 Lockout, when a coalition of Dublin employers faced down the new trade unionism of Jim Larkin. The Citizen Army was intended as a workers' defence body and, in the words of its co-founder Captain Jack White (a distinguished veteran of the Second Boer War), it amounted to 'the first Red Army in Europe.' Never numbering more than a few hundred men and women in its ranks, the Citizen Army's constitution boldly proclaimed that 'the ownership of Ireland, moral and material, is vested of right in the people of Ireland'. Liberty Hall, the headquarters of the Citizen Army, was proclaimed to be 'the brain of every riot and disturbance' in the city by *The Irish Times*.

They were joined by a range of other groupings, such as the women's organisation Cumann na mBan and the small Hibernian Rifles. Yet if the war provided the pretext for the rebels, British fears that the insurgents had acted in conjunction with Germany saw the Rising swiftly and ruthlessly suppressed, as troops flooded into Dublin and large tracts of the city were destroyed by artillery.

But this military defeat was transformed into a political victory for separatism by the British repression that followed: executions, mass internments and martial law, not to mention disillusionment with Ireland's traditional nationalist leaders and their support for an unpopular war, saw a political revolution in 1917–18 that radicalised nationalists into supporting a demand for full independence from Britain in the form of a vaguely defined republic. Take the case of

Ernie O'Malley, a young middle-class medical student from Mayo who wandered the streets of Dublin in bewilderment during the Easter Rising. By 1918, he was a full-time organiser with the Irish Republican Army, the guerrilla movement that emerged from the old Irish Volunteers. In the general election that followed the ending of the war, the newly revitalised Sinn Féin party (which had been erroneously blamed for the Rising) won most of Ireland's seats in Westminster. But the party boycotted the British parliament and established their own assembly in Dublin, Dáil Éireann, declaring Ireland independent as they did so.

The campaign of political resistance to British rule that followed over the next two and a half years went hand in hand with a military struggle: the Irish War of Independence. This conflict is often thought of in terms of the guerrilla war waged in rural Ireland, especially County Cork. But Dublin was a critical stage for the independence movement. It was the headquarters of that movement, it was the place that attracted the most obvious international attention, and to challenge the British on the streets of the Irish capital was deemed an essential task for both the politicians and administrators of Sinn Féin and the guerrillas of the IRA. Later still, Dublin would be a key theatre in the Civil War that accompanied the creation of an independent Irish state. And even aside from the succession of events, the experience of revolution was also shaped by issues that may not always have manifested themselves in dramatic events: the nationalist cultural revival of the Victorian and Edwardian eras, the struggles for economic and social justice on the part of the labour movement, and for the rights of Irishwomen on the part of the suffrage movement. Yet there is no shortage of locations in the Dublin that are associated with such campaigns and activities. The city was, in many ways, the hub of the Irish revolution and the venue for many of its iconic events. And many of the places in which that revolution was played out in the capital still exist.

This book is about those places and what happened in those places. The urban landscape of Dublin has changed in the last century, but much remains the same. It is possible to stand on Mount Street Bridge on the Grand Canal and make sense of the carnage that took place there as a column of British troops was ambushed there during the Easter Rising. Likewise, many buildings of importance to the story survive and are accessible to the public.

This book also includes places of commemoration and reflection, such as the Garden of Remembrance. These sites show us the manner in which the Irish state attempted to present the past in subsequent decades. For some, that state was the culmination of their efforts. To others (such as Helena Molony quoted above), it fell far short. Regardless of the paths eventually taken by those who took part in, witnessed or suffered in the Irish revolution, this book endeavours to shed light on the experience of life in Ireland's capital city in the course of that revolution.

1912 TIMELINE OF KEY EVENTS

11 APRIL: Introduction of Third Home Rule Bill in House of Commons by the Liberal government of Herbert Asquith, which will allow the establishment of a new devolved assembly in Dublin, with limited jurisdiction over all 32 Irish counties. This will be delayed by two years due to resistance in parliament.

11 JUNE: Amendment to Home Rule Bill proposes exclusion of counties Armagh, Antrim, Down and Londonderry from proposed Home Rule parliament in Dublin; this will evolve into the partition arrangement of 1920.

28 SEPTEMBER: 'Ulster Day', and signing of Solemn League and Covenant by over 237,000 men pledging to use 'all means which may be found necessary to defeat the present conspiracy to set up a Home Rule parliament in Ireland'; 234,000 women sign a declaration to the same effect.

1913

31 JANUARY: 31 January: Formation of Ulster Volunteer Force as a paramilitary body intended to resist the imposition of Home Rule.

7 JULY: The Home Rule Bill is finally passed by the House of Commons.

26 AUGUST: Beginning of Dublin Lockout, prompted by demands by Dublin employers banning membership of the Irish Transport and General Workers Union (ITGWU), founded by the charismatic Liverpool-born union leader James Larkin.

31 AUGUST: "Bloody Sunday": union members are brutally attacked throughout the city by the DMP following a banned rally on Sackville (O'Connell) Street, with a number of fatalities ensuing.

2 SEPTEMBER: Collapse of tenements in Church Street prompts outrage, and the establishment of an inquiry into Dublin's slum conditions.

19 NOVEMBER: Foundation of Irish Citizen Army as a trade union militia to protect striking workers during the Lockout.

25 NOVEMBER: A public meeting to establish and secure recruits to the Irish Volunteers takes place in Dublin's Rotunda Rink. This is in response to the creation of the UVF.

1914

18 JANUARY: Lockout officially ends.

20–21 MARCH: The 'Curragh incident' or 'Curragh mutiny', as large numbers of officers at the largest military base in Ireland offer to resign their commissions rather than be forced into action against the UVF should the British government seek to enforce Home Rule; they are given assurances that this will not happen. While no mutiny technically took place, the incident poses questions about the British commitment to Home Rule.

2 APRIL: Cumann na mBan is founded in Wynn's Hotel, Abbey St.

26 JULY: Howth gunrunning; a consignment of weapons bought in Germany is landed at the fishing port of Howth in north Dublin. After an abortive attempt by troops and the police to seize them, three people are shot dead by British troops on the Liffey quays.

4 AUGUST: German invasion of Belgium marks the beginning of the First World War and forces a British declaration of war.

9 SEPTEMBER: Irish Republican Brotherhood and other radicals meet in Dublin and decide to hold a rebellion before the end of the war, on the grounds that British involvement in the war offers too good an opportunity to pass up.

18 SEPTEMBER: Home Rule officially enacted but immediately suspended until the end of the war.

24 SEPTEMBER: Tensions in Irish Volunteers come to a head after the Home Rule leader, John Redmond, pledges his and his party's support to the British war effort, partly in order to secure British support for Home Rule. Eoin MacNeill, as leader of the Irish Volunteers, leads a split over the issue of supporting the war. The majority of the organisation follow Redmond and are renamed the Irish National Volunteers; the more militant faction that follow MacNeill retain the original name.

1915

1 AUGUST: The funeral of veteran republican Jeremiah O'Donovan Rossa in Glasnevin Cemetery, organised by the IRB and with a graveside oration by Patrick Pearse; this marks a public show of strength and a clear statement of intent by more militant separatist republicans.

6 AUGUST: 10th (Irish) Division lands at Gallipoli; Dublin recruits suffer heavy casualties in the initial landings.

1916

24–29 APRIL: The Easter Rising breaks out in Dublin and selected locations around the country. In all, 488 are killed in the fighting.

3–12 MAY: Fifteen men, including the leaders, are executed for their role in the Rising. All bar one are shot at Kilmainham Gaol in Dublin.

1 JULY: Battle of the Somme begins; the campaign will last until 18 November, with the British Army sustaining massive casualties.

22–23 DECEMBER: Release of untried – interned – 1916 prisoners from detention in Britain.

1917

5 FEBRUARY: Count George Plunkett, father of the executed 1916 leader Joseph Mary Plunkett, wins parliamentary by-election in Roscommon on a separatist ticket. This is the first of a number of by-elections won by republicans in 1917, indicating a shift in public support towards those who had fought in the Rising.

16 JUNE: All remaining 1916 prisoners, including Éamon de Valera, released from detention in Britain.

25 JULY: 'Irish convention' assembles in Trinity College Dublin. This round-table conference aimed at securing consensus between nationalists and unionists to secure the passage of Home Rule is fatally undermined as Ulster unionists decline to take part.

25/30 SEPTEMBER: Death and funeral of the 1916 leader Thomas Ashe, who dies after being forced-fed whilst on hunger strike. He is buried in Glasnevin Cemetery; the funeral is organised by the IRB, and provides another major show of strength for republicans in the capital.

25–27 OCTOBER: Sinn Féin annual convention in the Mansion House elects Éamon de Valera as leader of the newly reorganised party; the Irish Volunteers are reorganised at a meeting in Dublin at the same time.

1918

21 APRIL: Anti-conscription pledge signed nationwide in response to British willingness to impose conscription on Ireland; this is opposed by all shades of nationalist opinion, the Catholic Church and the labour movement, who organise a general strike in protest at conscription for 23 April.

10 OCTOBER: The sinking of the RMS *Leinster* by a U-boat just off Dublin Bay results in the death of 580 soldiers and civilians.

11 NOVEMBER: Armistice marks end of First World War.

14 DECEMBER: Polling opens for post-war general election on a greatly extended franchise that also grants women over 30 the right to vote in parliamentary elections for the first time. Sinn Fein win 73 seats but refuse to take them.

1919

21 JANUARY: Soloheadbeg attack in County Tipperary marks beginning of War of Independence; first meeting of first Dáil in Dublin's Mansion House declares Ireland independent.

28 JUNE: Treaty of Versailles signed, officially ending the First World War.

12 SEPTEMBER: Dáil Eireann declared illegal by British government.

25 NOVEMBER: Sinn Féin and Irish Volunteers declared illegal, having previously been suppressed.

19 DECEMBER: Attempted IRA assassination of Lord French, the incumbent viceroy, near Dublin's Phoenix Park.

1920

9 AUGUST: Restoration of Order in Ireland Act passed by British parliament, extending many of the extensive provisions of the wartime Defence of the Realm Act in Ireland and permitting the use of courts martial against the IRA.

20 SEPTEMBER: Sack of Balbriggan in County Dublin by British paramilitary police.

1 NOVEMBER: Execution of Kevin Barry in Mountjoy Gaol.

21 NOVEMBER: Bloody Sunday'; dozens killed in IRA attacks and British reprisals in Dublin and elsewhere.

23 DECEMBER: Government of Ireland Act enacted, formally partitioning Ireland into two jurisdictions and creating Northern Ireland.

1921

FEBRUARY–MARCH: Executions of IRA members take place in Cork and Dublin.

25 MAY: Destruction of Custom House in arson attack by the Dublin Brigade of the IRA.

9 JULY: Truce ends War of Independence.

6 DECEMBER: Anglo-Irish Treaty signed in London following extensive negotiations, establishing the Irish Free State.

14 DECEMBER: Dáil debates on the Treaty begin in the National University buildings in Dublin's Earlsfort Terrace.

1922

7 JANUARY: Treaty approved by Dáil, prompting an immediate split in the independence movement.

16 JANUARY: The new 'Provisional government' formally begins to take over power from British administration; British military withdrawal from southern Ireland subsequently commences.

14 APRIL: Four Courts occupied by anti-Treaty IRA.

24 APRIL: General strike against 'militarism' organised by labour movement, in protest at the prospect of looming Civil War.

28 JUNE: Attack on Four Courts and opening of hostilities in Dublin marks the beginning of the Civil War.

AUGUST: Deaths of Arthur Griffith (12 August) and Michael Collins (22 August). Both men are buried in Dublin's Glasnevin Cemetery, with both funerals being major public events attended by huge crowds.

5–6 DECEMBER: Irish Free State comes into existence.

8 DECEMBER: Executions of four anti-Treaty leaders in Mountjoy Prison.

1923

24 MAY : IRA ceasefire marks end of Civil War.

ABBREVIATIONS AND GLOSSARY

Auxiliaries: The Auxiliary Division of the Royal Irish Constabulary, recruited from veterans of the First World War. This was a separate paramilitary unit distinct from the RIC proper.

Black and Tans: The nickname given to special constabulary recruited from 1920 onward to bolster the ranks of the RIC, usually recruited, like the Auxiliaries, from First World War veterans. The name apparently derived from the mixture of police and army uniforms worn. They are often conflated with the Auxiliaries, and like them, they acquired a bad reputation for indiscipline and brutality.

BMH WS: Bureau of Military History Witness Statement. The bureau was established in the 1940s by the Irish government to compile a history of the independence movement. The witness statements were the oral testimonies collected from veterans.

Cumann na mBan: Founded in 1914 and loosely translated as Society or Association of Women. A distinct organisation in its own right, it was also intended to act as an adjunct to the Irish Volunteers.

DMP: Dublin Metropolitan Police; the unarmed police force for the Dublin area.

GAA: Gaelic Athletic Association, founded in 1884 to promote Irish sports over British sports such as soccer, rugby and cricket.

IPP: Irish Parliamentary Party, the main Irish constitutional national-ist party of the pre-independence era, demanding devolution for Ireland – Home Rule – within the UK.

IRA: Irish Republican Army. The paramilitary organisation that succeeded the Irish Volunteers and which was the principal group to fight British forces in the War of Independence. It split over the terms of the 1921 Treaty, with some members forming the core of the new National Army, while those hostile to the Treaty retained the name IRA.

IRB: Irish Republican Brotherhood. A secret conspiratorial body founded in the mid-nineteenth century to achieve Irish independence; it was responsible for planning the Easter Rising of 1916.

ITGWU: Irish Transport and General Workers' Union, founded by James Larkin in 1909.

Loyalist: A term denoting political allegiance to the British monarchy and state.

Republican: A term for an Irish separatist, as demands for Irish independence from Britain since the 1790s had generally been couched in terms of obtaining such independence in the form of a republic.

RIC: Royal Irish Constabulary, the armed police force responsible for policing outside Dublin.

Sinn Féin: Founded by Arthur Griffith in 1905, the name loosely translates as 'we ourselves'. It originally espoused a mixture of cultural and economic nationalism. The name was used as a catch-all term to describe more radical nationalists and the party was erroneously blamed for the Easter Rising. It was subsequently reorganised as an explicitly separatist party and became the primary republican organisation in the struggle for independence before it too split over the terms of the 1921 Treaty.

The 'Squad': The name given to the unit of the Dublin IRA tasked with carrying out assassinations. Drawn from the Dublin Brigade, the 'Squad' answered directly to Dick McKee and Michael Collins. Many of its former members became the core of the National Army's intelligence units during the Civil War.

Unionist: A term denoting a specific political position in favour of maintaining British rule in Ireland, in the form of the political union with the rest of the UK.

UVF: Ulster Volunteer Force; the overwhelmingly Protestant militia founded in 1913 in the north of Ireland to oppose the implementation of Home Rule.

HOW TO USE THIS BOOK

This book is arranged as a series of five walks, which taken together can amount to one much longer loop through the city. The book can therefore be used as a walking guide for one or all of the walks outlined. We cannot include every location associated with the revolution, but we have tried to include as many as we can within the limits of five reasonably easy walks, all of which can be completed in 90–120 minutes.

Many of the locations described here played multiple roles in the revolutionary period, but history and geography don't always overlap conveniently, so the book is not strictly chronological. Readers who want to keep the broad contours of the revolutionary period in mind are encouraged to refer to the outline of the revolution provided in the introduction. With regard to the individuals who shaped, witnessed or even became victims of the revolution, we have included some bio-graphical vignettes in the text where such individuals are the subject of a memorial, or were integral to what happened in given locations, and have included brief biographical notes on pages 187–195. We have also included extracts from contemporary accounts and eyewitness testimonies, some of which illustrate the stark and brutal reality of violence in the revolution. In addition, many street names redolent of British rule were changed after independence. For ease of use, we have generally opted for the street names in use today, rather than their pre-1922 counterparts.

The book can be dipped into as required to find out about specific locations. If you want to find out even more, we have included a list of sources and further reading, but bear in mind that many of these locations can be classed as visitor attractions and are open to the public. Opening times and admission prices (where applicable) can vary, so we have also listed the websites for many of the locations we visit in the book if you want to check in advance (see page 196).

Finally, we hope that this book can be read cover to cover, to pro-vide a short history of the Irish revolution in Dublin literally from the ground up.

NOTE ON SAFETY

If we were guiding you around the city, we would insist that you take the official pedestrian crossings. Be careful of traffic in the city centre at all times, and be careful of your footing if you stray off the footpaths. Be sure to wear the appropriate raingear and footwear. The authors and publisher accept no responsibility for any injuries, loss or inconvenience sustained by anyone using this book.

GETTING AROUND DUBLIN

Dublin city centre is easily navigated on foot, but the city as a whole is served by a number of public transport networks. The most extensive network is that of Dublin Bus: details on timetables and fares can be found at http://dublinbus.ie

The DART (Dublin Area Rapid Transit) line links the suburbs along the coast, and stops at a number of stations in the city centre: for full details of timetables and fares, see: http://www.irishrail.ie

The Luas tram network covers some of the more central suburbs, and the city centre itself: for details on timetables and fare, see: https://luas.ie

Dublin also has an extensive public bike-sharing scheme, with stops located throughout the city. See: www.dublinbikes.ie

The first stop on the first walk – Collins Barracks – can be accessed in a number of ways. From O'Connell Bridge, walk west along the north quays of the River Liffey; it is approximately a twenty-minute walk. The Luas Red Line stops outside the museum itself. If using Dublinbikes, the closest stop is at Smithfield. While no buses go directly to the museum, a number pass nearby. Numbers 37, 39, 39A and 70 travel up Blackhall Place and Manor Street, to the east of the museum, while buses serving Heuston Station pass the museum on the other side of the River Liffey: numbers 25, 25a, 25b, 66, 66a, 67, 69, 79, 79a, 145, 747. Simply get off at Heuston Station and the museum will be a five-minute walk away; it is clearly visible on the other side of the river from the station itself.

WALK 1 WESTERN APPROACHES

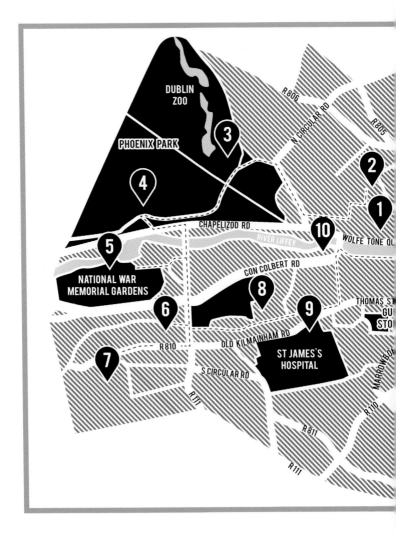

Introduction

At the start of the twentieth century the western fringes of Dublin were relatively sparsely populated; the creation of the vast western suburbs came after independence. Yet prior to 1922 this entire area of Dublin was, quite literally, a military and industrial complex, in that as well as the industrial areas created by railways and the enormous brewing quarters, many of the barracks and military installations in the city were concentrated west of the city and county and were particularly noticeable in this area.

1	COLLINS BARRACKS
2	ARBOUR HILL
3	PHOENIX PARK
4	THE MAGAZINE FORT AND THE FIFTEEN ACRES
5	NATIONAL WAR MEMORIAL GARDENS
6	KILMAINHAM GAOL
7	RICHMOND BARRACKS
8	ROYAL HOSPITAL KILMAINHAM
9	SOUTH DUBLIN UNION
10	DR STEEVENS' HOSPITAL AND HEUSTON STATION
11	THE GUINNESS BREWERY AND THE MENDICITY INSTITUTION

1 COLLINS BARRACKS

W e begin at Collins Barracks (formerly the Royal Barracks), originally built in the first decade of the eighteenth century and, at the time of its construction, the largest barracks in Europe. It was built at a time when the British Army was becoming more formally structured, and the British government felt the need to keep their army out of sight and out of mind in Ireland rather than have it based in Britain itself. Throughout its history, it was the largest barracks in Ireland, and could apparently accommodate 5,000 infantry and cavalry. Originally, there were three 'squares', only two of which survive; some of the buildings were removed at the end of the nineteenth century for sanitary purposes. Since the construction of the barracks in the 1700s, this area was strongly associated with the military. Much of the area around Collins Barracks contained businesses, industries and institutions directly related to the military presence in the area. Prostitution was also common here in the nineteenth century.

During the First World War, members of the Royal Dublin Fusiliers who served in the Gallipoli Campaign (February 1915 – January 1916) were trained here, and amongst those in the barracks during the Easter Rising were the first British soldiers ordered into action during the Rising. The officer assumed to be the first 'British' military casualty in 1916, Gerald Neilan of the Royal Dublin Fusiliers, was killed by gunfire on the quays as he and his troops left the barracks to move into the city as the Rising began. Neilan was, in fact, Irish and, ironically, his younger brother Arthur was serving with the Irish Volunteers in and around the Four Courts. The barracks was occupied by the British Army until December 1922; its garrison was the last to leave Dublin after the foundation of the Irish Free State, and the complex was subsequently renamed Collins Barracks.

WALK 1, STOP 1 ■

*Collins Barracks, formerly the Royal Barracks and now
the National Museum of Ireland (Decorative Arts & History).
(Courtesy Dennis Horgan)*

2 ARBOUR HILL

L eave Collins Barracks via the ramp leading to the rear entrance near the old Riding School (which houses the yacht *Asgard*, used to smuggle weapons in to Howth for the Irish Volunteers in July 1914), and cross the road to Arbour Hill prison. It was built in the 1840s as a military prison, and was one of a number of military installations used to detain republican prisoners after the Easter Rising; it also housed prisoners during the War of Independence and the Civil War. It is still in use as a prison, but the grounds of the church adjacent to the prison are open. The church itself would have been the garrison chapel for the nearby barracks; as such, it is one of the oldest military chapels in Ireland. The military graveyard alongside was chosen as the location for the graves of the fourteen men executed in Dublin for their involvement in the Rising, including the seven signatories of the Proclamation. All were buried in a mass grave with quicklime. Remarkably precise instructions were issued for the burials, which took place in the exercise yard of the prison, out of public view. This was a deliberate decision to minimise any propaganda value that the graves might have: as the military governor, General Sir John Maxwell, observed, 'Irish sentimentality will turn these graves into martyrs' shrines'. The burial plot was laid out in its current form by Office of Public Works in 1956, and incorporates a limestone wall with the text of the 1916 Proclamation in both Irish and English.

3 PHOENIX PARK

O n leaving Arbour Hill Prison, turn right along Arbour Hill. The first right turn is Cavalry Row, which gives a view of St Bricin's Military Hospital (formerly the King George V Hospital, completed in 1913; the bodies of Dick McKee and Peadar Clancy, who were killed by British forces on Bloody Sunday 1920, were brought here after their deaths. Continue on and turn left when you reach the junction with St Bricin's Park and following the hill south until you turn right onto Montpelier Hill. At the end of Montpelier Hill is Infirmary Road, so called after the old Royal Infirmary located across the road, to your left. This was later the headquarters of the British military establishment in Ireland; it currently houses the Irish Department of Defence. Turn right to travel north along Infirmary Road, and turn left at the gate to enter the Phoenix Park.

The Phoenix Park was originally laid out as a royal deer park in the 1670s, and has its own set of military installations and military associations. Follow the road around to the left. Pausing at the first junction, to your right you will see the squat granite buildings of the Garda Headquarters; formerly the Royal Irish Constabulary Headquarters Depot, it was built in the 1840s. In the decades prior to the First World War, members of various colonial police forces were trained here for service in other parts of the British Empire. Given that the Black and Tans and Auxiliaries of the War of Independence were technically police officers, the depot was used by them in 1920–21 as well. If you were to take the path across the front of the depot, the enormous Victorian edifice of Marlborough Barracks, now McKee Barracks, can be seen. This is one of the most remarkable collections of Victorian buildings in the city and prior to independence was a cavalry barracks from which troops who served and fought in the Easter Rising were dispatched in April 1916. However, its elaborate buildings are best seen from Blackhorse Avenue off the North Circular Road rather than from the park.

Continue along North Road towards the junction with Chesterfield Avenue. On your left is the People's Flower Garden, and just inside its railings you will see a large memorial statue by Laurence Campbell of the executed 1916 leader Seán Heuston, unveiled in December 1943. Heuston was from Dublin's inner city and, like many Dubliners who fought in the Easter Rising, was a graduate of the Christian Brothers O'Connell Schools, and in 1907 became a clerk in the Great Southern and Western Railway (GSWR). He was stationed in the Limerick depot, and while there he moved into the circles of 'advanced' nationalism. He joined the Irish Republican Brotherhood (IRB) and the republican boy-scout movement Na Fianna Éireann, the organisation with which he was most closely identified. Heuston rose through the ranks and joined the Irish Volunteers after his return to Dublin in 1913 to work at the GSWR depot at Kingsbridge (later renamed Heuston Station after him). He led a small detachment to seize the

Mendicity Institution on Usher's Island during the 1916 Rising; he was executed for his role and is buried in the plot on Arbour Hill.

Continue along until you get to Chesterfield Avenue, the main avenue through the Phoenix Park. The view to the left, looking back towards the city, frames the buildings of the Guinness Brewery and also the spire of St Patrick's Cathedral. Take care crossing the avenue, as there is no official crossing, and continue to follow the road, now called Wellington Road. On your left is the enormous Wellington Testimonial, proposed in 1813 and completed in 1861 to a design by Robert Smirke in tribute to Arthur Wellesley, Duke of Wellington, who was born just off Merrion Square (it was officially designated a testimonial rather than a memorial, as Wellington was still alive when it was commissioned). It is the largest obelisk in Europe, and is located on what would have been the old salute battery in the park, used throughout the eighteenth and nineteenth centuries for firing artillery salutes. The plates on the sides of the monuments depict battles and campaigns in which Wellington would have fought and also Wellington's alleged role in the granting of Catholic emancipation in 1829. It was supposed to have been surrounded by a set of structures, but these were never completed. While not immediately relevant to the revolutionary era, the 67-metre-high monument is hard to miss and is another indication of this area's traditional association with the British military.

■ **WALK 1, STOP 4**
The Magazine Fort in Phoenix Park.
(Courtesy Dennis Horgan)

4 | THE MAGAZINE FORT AND THE FIFTEEN ACRES

By continuing on the road, you come to a hollow and, at the top of its rim, the Magazine Fort, originally completed in 1738 and renovated thereafter, and worth the short climb to see; there are grass paths leading up to it, but if you continue along the road you will come to an access road with a footpath. Unsupervised access to the building is restricted. The military barracks in Dublin tended to be in the west of the city, given that strategically attacks on Dublin were likely to come from the west, and the sea acted as a natural barrier to the east. On eighteenth-century maps, there were plans for an enormous star fort in this area. That was never built, but the much smaller Magazine Fort was constructed instead, and the enormous, expansive land to its west, the so-called Fifteen Acres (which is obviously much bigger than 15 acres), was used for artillery practice and military reviews throughout the eighteenth and nineteenth centuries. Indeed, during the First World War, trenches were dug in the Fifteen Acres to act as a training venue for soldiers being dispatched to the front.

The Magazine Fort is an impressive vantage point overlooking the park and much of the surrounding area, with the Royal Hospital Kilmainham and the National War Memorial Gardens at Islandbridge being visible; a grass path runs around the perimeter, though be careful of the edge of the ditch that surrounds the fort as there is no guard rail.

Before leaving the Magazine Fort, look west across the Fifteen Acres and in the distance you will see a set of grey buildings: the Royal Hibernian Military School. The Hibernian Society for the Orphans and Widows of Soldiers was originally founded in 1765, and the buildings opened in 1771. It took in boys only from 1846 and was effectively a military school; it had many non-Irish students due to the stationing of non-Irish units in Dublin, and many of its students subsequently enlisted in the British Army. In all, 1,250 former students fought in the First World War, and 82 were killed. It was due to host a reunion on 24 April 1916, the day on which the Easter Rising broke out.

The Magazine Fort is particularly associated with the Easter Rising as there was an unsuccessful attempt to seize its arsenal when the Rising began. This happened in the guise of a football match, which gave members of the Irish Volunteers an excuse to get close to the gate of the fort. They rushed the gate and managed to escape with some weapons and ammunition.

To continue on the route, retrace your steps down the hill and head towards the Islandbridge gate of the park. The attractive Victorian gate lodge on the left was the scene of a killing during the attack on the Magazine Fort. Arthur Playfair, the 23-year-old son of the gate keeper (not a younger son as is sometimes claimed), ran towards the lodge to raise the alarm. Garry Holohan of Na Fianna Éireann pursued him on a bike and shot him on the doorstep. Playfair later died of his wounds. The lodge is a private residence.

We took the guards' rifles and went to the waiting hackney car ... I followed behind the car on my bicycle. As the car turned towards the gate leading to the Chapelizod Road we noticed a youth of about seventeen years of age running towards the gate. He stopped and spoke to the policeman who was in the middle of the road directing the traffic, and then ran away in the middle of the road towards

Islandbridge. I left the hack and followed him, and when he got to the corner of Islandbridge Road he ran towards one of the big houses, evidently with the intention of giving the alarm. I jumped off my bicycle, and just as the door opened I shot him from the gate.

Garry Holohan describes the immediate aftermath of the raid on the Magazine Fort. Military Archives BMH WS 328.

Exit the gate, turn left and then turn right again to cross the River Liffey over the bridge, staying on the right-hand path. The remains of Clancy Barracks, formerly Islandbridge Barracks and now converted into apartments, will be visible to your left on the other side of the bridge. This was part of the ring of military installations in the area, and in this case, an artillery barracks whose troops often practised in the Fifteen Acres.

5 | NATIONAL WAR MEMORIAL GARDENS

Continue south; on the right is a flat complex, the car park of which offers access to the National War Memorial Gardens, which are signposted. Turn right and continue along the path until you come to the gate of the gardens. While the First World War did not come to Dublin except perhaps in the form of the Easter Rising, the impact of the war and the impact of Ireland's associations with the British military can be seen throughout this area of west Dublin. The erection of a national memorial to Irish servicemen who had served in the Great War was being proposed almost as soon as the war was over; in 1919 a trust fund was established to that end. There were various suggestions as to what form such a memorial would take (such as a physical monument, or some form of practical assistance to ex-servicemen). Political sensitivities arising from the struggle for independence complicated the issue, but a physical memorial was ultimately settled upon, though its form and location were still up for debate. Merrion Square was one possible venue, but the prospect of erecting a war memorial there was dismissed by the Free State Minister for Justice, Kevin O'Higgins, who had lost a brother in the war but who went on to point out that such a memorial located beside Leinster House could give the misleading impression that the war had led to Irish independence, rather than the independence struggle itself: 'No one

■ **WALK 1, STOP 5**
The War Memorial Gardens in Islandbridge. (Courtesy Dennis Horgan)

denies the sacrifice, and no one denies the patriotic motives which induced the vast majority of those men to join the British Army to take part in the Great War, and yet it is not on their sacrifice that this state is based, and I have no desire to see it suggested that it is'. O'Higgins was also wary of its potential exploitation for political purposes, an ongoing concern.

The trustees of the war memorial project had, by the late 1920s, lost interest in a city-centre site for a memorial, and instead began to focus on the Phoenix Park, which had become the major Dublin venue for the commemoration of Armistice Day. This was partly due to the fact that the police had banned parades on 11 November, traditionally held in College Green, due to their potential for public disorder; but it is also a testament to the sheer scale of Armistice Day events, which were often attended by tens of thousands of people. The Phoenix Park was proposed as a possible venue by Sir Bryan Mahon, the former commander of the 10th (Irish) Division, as it could accommodate the large crowds that continued to commemorate Armistice Day until the outbreak of the Second World War.

In December 1929 a site in Islandbridge was chosen. The trustees of the memorial campaign, headed by Sir Andrew Jameson, pledged £54,000 and the government pledged £50,000. In an ecumenical gesture, the labour to build the site was to be drawn evenly from former veterans of both the British armed forces and the National Army. The memorial was designed by Sir Edwin Lutyens, the architect of the London Cenotaph, and consisted of landscaped gardens that swept down to the River Liffey's edge, where you will find a domed pavilion, on the floor of which is an inscription from the war poet Rupert Brooke.

To reach the main section of the memorial, take the path directly south from the gazebo and climb the steps. Here, there are four pavilions that were intended to house records of the dead, along with a number of large fountains and, acting as centrepieces, a 'stone of remembrance' and a large Celtic cross. The central stone, also designed by Lutyens, is a standard memorial used by the Commonwealth War Graves Commission throughout the world (though they do not administer the Islandbridge gardens). The memorial was completed between 1931–38 (a planned bridge over the Liffey was abandoned as too expensive). The construction straddled the change of government in 1932: Éamon de Valera was supportive of the project and had planned to open the memorial formally in 1939, but this was postponed indefinitely due to the outbreak of the Second World War. The gardens fell into disrepair over time and were not officially opened until 1 July 2006, the ninetieth anniversary of the Battle of the Somme.

While its slightly peripheral location is sometimes used as a metaphor for the marginalisation of the Great War in Irish public life (prior to the 1990s anyway), the fact remains that the National War Memorial Gardens at Islandbridge are unique: they remain the largest monument to military service of any description on the island of Ireland. However, the figure of over 49,000 dead inscribed near the memorial cross is almost certainly incorrect; the number of Irish-born dead in the First World War is closer to 35,000.

6 KILMAINHAM GAOL

The most attractive way to exit the gardens is to retrace your steps out to the road and walk south up the hill, crossing the busy main road with care and continuing on to the next T-junction. On the left is the Royal Hospital Kilmainham (now IMMA, the Irish Museum of Modern Art) and on the right will be Kilmainham Gaol, originally built in the 1790s as the Dublin County Jail, and which has more obvious links to the revolutionary period than its neighbour. The original main entrance is adorned with an elaborate carving of a hydra, intended to symbolise disorder. Ironically, it had closed prior to the First World War, but was reopened in the aftermath of the Easter Rising of 1916 to accommodate republican prisoners, and this is what gives it an enduring reputation. As well as housing the prisoners of the Easter Rising, Kilmainham was also the venue for the execution of 14 of the 16 men executed after the Rising (only Thomas Kent in Cork and Roger Casement in London were executed elsewhere).

WALK 1, STOP 6

Above: The west wing of Kilmainham Gaol;
Left: commemorative plaque in the Stonebreakers' Yard,
Kilmainham Gaol. (Courtesy Las Fallon)

▌ *At 3.45 the first rebel MacDonoghue* [sic] *was marched in blind-folded, and the firing party placed 10 paces distant. Death was instantaneous. The second, P.H. Pierce* [sic] *whistled as he came out of the cell ... The same applied to him. The third, J.H. Clarke* [sic]*, an old man, was not quite so fortunate, requiring a bullet from the officer to complete the ghastly business (it was sad to think that these three brave men who met their death so bravely should be fighting for a cause which proved so useless and had been the means of so much bloodshed).* ▌

Sergeant-Major Samuel Lomas of the Sherwood Foresters recalls the executions of Thomas MacDonagh, Patrick Pearse and Thomas Clarke in the yard of Kilmainham Gaol after the Easter Rising, 3 May 1916: Mick O'Farrell (ed.), The 1916 Diaries of an Irish Rebel and a British Soldier *(Cork, 2014).*

Kilmainham Gaol played a role throughout the subsequent War of Independence, when it was used to house prisoners. In February 1921 three prisoners – Simon Donnelly, Ernie O'Malley and Frank Teeling (the latter was apparently under sentence of death) – escaped with the aid of a sympathetic soldier, who had smuggled in a bolt cutter that was used to cut open one of the gates. Kilmainham remained in use as a prison during the Civil War when many inmates went on hunger strike; a number of executions of anti-Treaty IRA members also took place there. It closed for good in 1924 but from the 1960s was restored by volunteer projects, very often including volunteers who were themselves veterans of the independence struggle. It was renovated again in 2016 as part of the centenary commemorations of the Easter Rising.

7 | RICHMOND BARRACKS

S lightly north-west of Kilmainham in Inchicore is Richmond Barracks, opened in 1815 during the Napoleonic Wars; the location had the useful consequence of drawing soldiers who tended to be notoriously ill-disciplined out of the city centre and therefore keeping them out of trouble. To get there, continue along the South Circular Road, turning left at Emmet Road. Continue until you reach St Michael's Church (originally the garrison church), and turn left onto Bulfin Road and right onto St Michael's Estate, which is where the remains of Richmond Barracks are located. It was active as a barracks up to the 1920s, though only one portion of the original structure survives. The remaining buildings would have comprised the eastern side of the central square. During the First World War, the poet Francis Ledwidge spent time in the barracks after enlisting in the British Army. Richmond was a key venue for housing prisoners after the Easter Rising, including 77 women who participated in the Rebellion. The courts martial that condemned those executed in the aftermath of the Rising to death also took place here; it was handed over to the National Army in 1922, along with the other Dublin barracks vacated by the British.

> *One day (I don't remember whether it was Monday or Tuesday, 1st or 2nd of May) a number of us were taken to be charged by the court ... While we were waiting to go in, we sat on the grass outside. The guards sat down too and an argument developed about the merits of the Rising. I ventured a remark and one of the guards, a red-haired Irishman, said "You shut up, you Scotch bastard. You only came over here to make trouble."*

> *John McGallogly, from Glasgow, recalls awaiting court martial at Richmond Barracks. Military Archives BMH WS 244.*

Adjacent to the barracks is Goldenbridge Cemetery, opened in 1828 by the Dublin Cemeteries Committee, which would open Prospect – Glasnevin – Cemetery a few years later. This is a small but surprisingly intact Victorian cemetery, which was closed in the 1860s after the British Army complained that it was causing a health hazard in the vicinity of the barracks. Burials were still allowed in the cemetery, however, as long as they were of family members of those already interred there, though it has recently been reopened.

■ **WALK 1, STOP 7**

Above: Major John MacBride at Richmond Barracks. (Courtesy Richmond Barracks)

Far Right: Female participants in the Easter Rising, including members of Cumann na mBan and the Irish Citizen Army, photographed in its aftermath. Notice the copy of Irish War News, *produced during the Rising. (Courtesy Richmond Barracks)*

It houses a number of graves relating to the Easter Rising, including that of W.T. Cosgrave, the Sinn Féin alderman and Irish Volunteer officer who was second in command of the Irish Volunteers at the nearby South Dublin Union and who was later the first premier of the Irish Free State. Also buried in Goldenbridge is Cosgrave's stepbrother Frank Burke, who was killed at the South Dublin Union in 1916.

8 ROYAL HOSPITAL KILMAINHAM

Retracing your steps back to Kilmainham Gaol, cross the road and enter the grounds of the Royal Hospital Kilmainham. It was originally built in the 1680s as a rest home for old and injured soldiers based on Les Invalides in Paris, which was a function it continued to fulfil well into the 1920s. It was a military installation and was General Sir John Maxwell's military headquarters during the Easter Rising of 1916; machine-gun positions on the south side of the building were used to fire on the insurgent positions in and around the nearby South Dublin Union. It remains one of Dublin's finest and indeed oldest significant surviving public buildings. It was used for various military purposes throughout this period. Indeed, on 12 July 1921 – the day after the Truce that ended the War of Independence – the hospital hosted a ceremony, with full regimental bands and a guard of honour, awarding 26 citations for bravery in combat with the IRA in Ireland. The last of its residents left in 1927, after which it became the Garda headquarters. The large arch at the main entrance originally stood on the south quays of the River Liffey, and on the main avenue are two cemeteries: on your left, as you approach the main building, is Bully's Acre, reputedly the oldest cemetery in the city, while there is a small military cemetery on the other side of the avenue.

■ **WALK 1, STOP 8**
The area around Mount Brown and the south inner city as seen from the Royal Hospital Kilmainham in the 1950s. The two tall buildings in the background are part of the Guinness Brewery, while the longer dormitories visible in the foreground are part of the South Dublin Union. (Courtesy of Bureau of Military History, Military Archives, Cathal Brugha Barracks)

9 | SOUTH DUBLIN UNION

Continue through the main building, cross the courtyard and exit the ground through the rear gate, turning left onto Bow Street. Cross over the River Camac and take the steps on your right – officially called Cromwell's Quarters, and once called 'Murdering Lane'. At the top of the lane is Mount Brown, and directly across the road from the top of the steps are some of the few remaining buildings of what was once the South Dublin Union, the scene of the some of the most intense fighting to take place in Dublin during the Easter Rising in 1916.

The South Dublin Union was Ireland's largest workhouse, housing 3,200 inmates in a sprawling complex that covered 50 acres; its catchment area was the largest of any of Ireland's numerous poor law unions. It was administered by a board of guardians largely composed of Home Rulers, who had been criticised by the labour movement for their perceived hostility to unions in 1911 and for alleged corruption and mismanagement that resulted in poor conditions and diets for the malnourished inmates. These allegations continued into 1913 and were not without foundation. The seizure of such a large complex would have enabled the Volunteers to impede the movement of troops from Richmond Barracks. It was taken by the 4th Battalion of the Dublin Volunteers under Eamonn Ceannt, who assembled in the Liberties before moving along Cork Street to seize the complex.

> *One of the sentry posts was in the corridor of the Nurses' Home commanding a view of the open space, the rectangle of the Protestant church and dining hall. He was a section commander, C/Company, Frank (Gobbon) Burke, and particularly keen on his work and duty as a Volunteer. Across the road from where he was on duty a wing of the hospital was on about the same level. An enemy soldier got into the hospital, saw young Frank Burke, took aim and shot him through the throat. He died immediately, R.I.P.*

> W.T. Cosgrave recalls the fighting in the South Dublin Union and the death of his stepbrother, Frank Burke. Military Archives BMH WS 268.

A number of outlying buildings were also seized in this area, such as Watkins Brewery in Ardee Street, the Jameson Distillery in Marrowbone Lane, and Roe's Distillery in Mount Brown, which was located to the right of the top of the steps (the Volunteers declined to sample any of their wares). There was no attempt made to seize Kingsbridge (Heuston) Station, which was a major oversight. The South Dublin Union was the site of intense fighting on Monday 24 April, Tuesday 25 April and Thursday 27 April; this

The entrance to the South Dublin Union on James's Street, pictured in the 1950s. The upper windows belonged to a boardroom that was occupied during the Easter Rising. (Courtesy of Bureau of Military History, Military Archives, Cathal Brugha Barracks)

is where Cathal Brugha earned his reputation for bravery, by continuing to fight despite being badly wounded. Part of the complex was occupied by British troops, but their attention shifted elsewhere as the week went on. The site is now the location of St James's Hospital. Only a small number of the original buildings survive, but the housing estate to the west of the remaining buildings is called Ceannt Fort; a small tribute to the leader of the Volunteer garrison.

■ **WALK 1, STOP 10**
*Graves of Irish Volunteers and
British soldiers sit side by side at
the rear of Dr Steevens' Hospital.*

10 DR STEEVENS' HOSPITAL AND HEUSTON STATION

Continue east along James's Street until you come to the Luas line; turn left, taking the path to follow the tramline down to the end of the hill. At the bottom, on the left, is Dr Steevens' Hospital, originally completed in the 1730s and a now a facility owned by the Health Service Executive. It retains a small military cemetery, in which are buried both British and Irish Volunteer casualties of the Easter Rising. It also had another role in revolutionary Dublin: in early 1919 it was the venue for a new special treatment centre for sexually transmitted diseases, which were prevalent enough in a city with high levels of prostitution but which seem to have spiked as demobilised soldiers returned home from the war. Across the road from the hospital is Kingsbridge – now Heuston – Station, built in the 1840s as the principal depot for the Great Southern and Western Railway (GSWR), one of the largest of Ireland's rail companies; its lines, covering the south and west of the country, comprised a third of the total Irish rail network by the turn of the twentieth century, and Kingsbridge was the largest rail depot in the country. The wings on each side of the main palazzo concourse, which vaguely resemble locomotives, are notable. Like many of the major businesses of Edwardian Ireland, the GWSR management were unionist in political outlook, and during the First World War members of staff were encouraged to enlist. A bronze roll of honour, commemorating those employees killed in the war, is located on the south concourse of the station.

Éirí Amach na Cásca 1916

I gcuimhne Bhriogáid Átha Cliath, Óglaigh na hÉireann
In memory of the Dublin Brigade, Irish Volunteers

Commandant Seán Heuston (Executed 8 May)

An Chéad Chathlán 1st Battalion	5ú Cathlán (Fine Gall) 5th Battalion (Fingal)
Capt. Richard Balfe	Capt. Richard Coleman
James Brennan	John Clarke
Frederick Brooks	James Crenigan
John J Byrne	Patrick J Kelly
Frank Cullen	Richard Kelly
Seán Derrington	James Marks
William Derrington	William Meehan
George Levins	Joseph Norton
Seán McLoughlin	Thomas Peppard
William Murnane	Peter Wilson
William O'Dea	James Wilson
Thomas O'Kelly	William Wilson
Edward Roach	Peter Wilson †
Liam Staines†	
Patrick J Stephenson	

a throid ar son Shaoirse na hÉireann ag Institiúid Mendicity
who fought at the Mendicity Institution for Irish freedom

24 – 26 Aibreán / April
1916 Easter Rising

Cast Ltd, Dub

WALK 1, STOP 11
*Commemorative plaque
at Mendicity Institution
(Courtesy Las Fallon)*

Kingsbridge played a role in the Easter Rising. At around 4.45pm on Monday 24 April, troop reinforcements from the Curragh began to disembark at the station, and some of these were sent on to the North Wall via the loop line to reinforce the docks. As Easter Week wore on, the rail workshops were used to convert five Daimler trucks, which had been borrowed from the Guinness Brewery, into impromptu armoured cars; two had locomotive boilers fixed to the chassis, with loopholes for guns cut into the metal. They were used to ferry troops and supplies around the city, while one was used in the controversial capture of North King Street later in the week. The station was renamed Heuston in 1966 after Seán Heuston, whose statue we saw earlier in the Phoenix Park.

11 THE GUINNESS BREWERY AND THE MENDICITY INSTITUTION

Leave Heuston Station and walk east along the south quays, with Collins Barracks on the other side of the river. What will be obvious here is the presence of the rather large premises of a rather well-known company, located in this part of the city since 1759. The enormous Guinness Brewery was, at the turn of the twentieth century, the largest in the world, and the revolution impinged upon the company in numerous ways. During the Easter Rising, troops would occupy some of the buildings, and a bizarre incident took place in which a number of soldiers and civilians were killed in a case of mistaken identity. Its more enduring legacy, however, was as a source of soldiers to serve with the British Army during the First World War. The Guinness family, like many of the business elites of Ireland at this stage, would have been unionists, as were many of their employees, many of whom served in the First World War and many of whom were killed. This was a phenomenon that could be seen amongst many of the old established companies, such as the railway companies that existed in the Ireland of 1912 to 1923.

The First World War put pressure on brewers, as markets were cut off and supplies were scarce, and government restrictions were imposed on the drinks industry. To their credit, Guinness declined to profiteer from the supply of animal feed left over from brewing to dairies. Guinness offered to keep jobs for soldiers that enlisted during the war; over 650 employees fought and 104 were killed. Those who served were kept on half pay, and many were re-employed after the war; the firm even employed soldiers with wounds that restricted their working ability, though in 1922 some of those deemed unfit were let go (pre-war employees were given an allowance). Hundreds of ex-service men were re-employed, leading to the justifiable perception that such veterans were favoured. But National Army and even IRA members were also re-employed by the firm after the war, though the traditional affiliations of the firm were shown by the fact that the 11 November two-minute silence was regularly observed in the brewery and the company premises.

Continue along the quays until you come to the distinctive white James Joyce Bridge, designed by Santiago Calatrava. The design of the bridge, with its two arches leaning out, is supposed to evoke the pages of a book, because the building facing the bridge on the south side of the River Liffey is the Georgian house that was the setting for Joyce's legendary short story 'The Dead'. Directly east of the house is the location of the Mendicity Institution, a charity founded in 1819 to deal with the problem of begging in Dublin by providing schooling, training and meals to Dublin's urban poor: in 1916 alone it served meals to over 16,000 people. The building in which it was originally housed, and which was occupied in 1916, was built in the 1750s as the townhouse of the Earls of Moira, who sold it after the 1801 Act of Union. It was located on the southern side of the River Liffey at Usher's Island, on the edge of the vast complex of distilleries and breweries based in that part of the city. The building was occupied by members of the Irish Volunteers led by Seán Heuston, who was later executed for his role in the Rising. The building was chosen due its location on the Liffey Quays: Heuston and those under his command were to ambush any soldiers who might be mobilised from the Royal Barracks (now Collins Barracks) on the other side of the river. This was to enable other members of the Volunteers to establish positions around Church Street and the Four Courts without fear of attack. The original building has been demolished but the outer wall survives.

Continue east past the Mendicity Institution and turn left onto Bridgefoot Street, travelling up the hill. At the top of the hill, cross the road to get to St Catherine's, formerly a Church of Ireland church. Outside the church is a memorial to the republican Robert Emmet, who was executed at this spot in September 1803 for attempting to stage an abortive rebellion. The preparations for Emmet's rebellion had been firmly rooted in this part of the city; weapons had been surreptitiously prepared in secret depots, and some of the proposed assembly points were nearby.

The site of his execution had a natural resonance for Irish nationalists and republicans. When the funeral cortège of the 1916 leader Thomas Ashe left City Hall to make its way to Glasnevin Cemetery on 30 September 1917, it took a circuitous route to maximise the propaganda value, and made a point of passing the site of Emmet's execution to forge a symbolic link between one generation of republicans and another.

To begin the second walk, stay on Thomas Street and walk east towards the city centre. Upon reaching Christ Church cathedral, turn right and continue along Patrick's Street until you reach St Patrick's Cathedral.

WALK 2

THE SOUTH-WEST INNER CITY

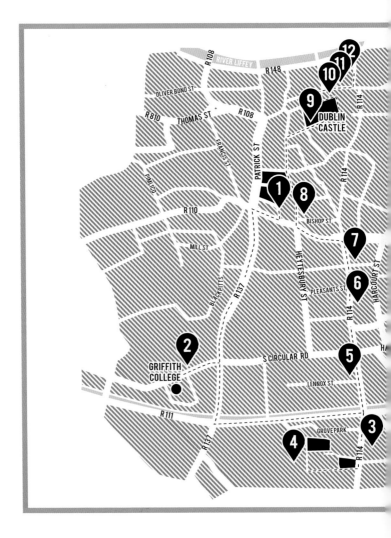

Introduction

The second walk follows a route that ranges from the fringes of medieval Dublin out towards the suburban townships that began to emerge in the Victorian era. In doing so, it follows a route that is explicitly associated with the military conflict that shaped the Irish revolution from 1916 to 1923, before ending up in some locations that are associated with the ideologies and political beliefs that motivated and underpinned the conflict.

1 MARSH'S LIBRARY

2 GRIFFITH COLLEGE

3 CHURCH OF OUR LADY OF REFUGE, RATHMINES

4 PORTOBELLO BARRACKS

5 PORTOBELLO AND LENNOX STREET

6 CAMDEN STREET

7 ROBERT TRESSELL PLAQUE, WEXFORD STREET

8 JACOB'S FACTORY

9 DUBLIN CASTLE

10 CITY HALL

11 BLOODY SUNDAY PLAQUE, EXCHANGE COURT

12 QUAKER MEETING HOUSE AND PLAQUE TO UNITED IRISHMEN

1 MARSH'S LIBRARY

We begin outside one of Dublin's two cathedrals; St Patrick's is the younger of the two, and was originally located outside Dublin's medieval walls, though like its counterpart, Christ Church, it is a cathedral of the Church of Ireland. While most commonly associated with Jonathan Swift, the eighteenth-century dean of the cathedral who wrote, amongst other things, *Gulliver's Travels*, the interior of St Patrick's offers a striking set of memorials to Irish military service in the British armed forces over the centuries. With regards to the revolutionary period, our first port of call is not the cathedral but the modest-looking building adjacent to it. Walk away from Patrick's Street, passing the main entrance to the cathedral, following St Patrick's Close and you will come to a gate that leads to a squat building: this is Marsh's Library, originally established in 1707 by Narcissus Marsh, the Church of Ireland Archbishop of Dublin. In the early years of the First World War, some members of the library staff enlisted. During the Rising the building suffered damage when it was machine-gunned from St Patrick's Park by British troops on the morning of 30 April. The reason is unclear. The library authorities deemed the gunfire to have been an accident. Five books from the original eighteenth-century collection of the first librarian of Marsh's Library, the French Huguenot Elias Bouhéreau, were damaged, as was some of the internal woodwork. During the Rising the library lost another 40 books that had been sent to a bookbinder on Abbey Street; they were destroyed in the fires around O'Connell Street. The windows of Marsh's were also damaged during the Civil War in October 1922, in an act deemed to be sectarian by the library authorities.

Continue to the end of the close and turn right onto Kevin Street, passing the Garda station. This was the archiepiscopal palace of St Sepulchre, originally built as the residence of John Cumin, Archbishop of Dublin from 1181 to 1212. It has been heavily rebuilt over the centuries and from 1836 was the headquarters of the Dublin Metropolitan Police. Continue to the junction with New Street and turn left. Walking away from the city, you will pass Fumbally Lane and Malpas Street, both on the right-hand side of the street; small Volunteer outposts from the republican garrison in the Jacob's factory were established here briefly during the Easter Rising, but after a matter of hours they were forced out by hostile locals; this area (the 'Liberties') was an area in which recruitment to the British Army was high, and the families of serving soldiers were hostile to the insurgents. The Volunteers killed three people in the stand-offs that took place in and around these streets, including fifteen-year-old Eleanor Warbrook of Malpas Terrace, one of over 40 children killed in the Rising. It should be said that Patrick Street, New Street and Clanbrassil Street (all of which form part of the same thoroughfare) are much wider now than they were then and have been heavily redeveloped over time.

Continue along New Street and Clanbrassil Street to the junction with the South Circular Road at Leonard's Corner.

2 GRIFFITH COLLEGE

Turn right at Leonard's Corner and continue for about 100 metres. If you think the nineteenth-century building on the other side of the road vaguely resembles a prison, you would be right, for that is what it once was. Griffith College originally opened in 1813 as the Richmond Bridewell. It was designed by Francis Johnston, the architect of the GPO. Amongst its nineteenth-century inmates were Daniel O'Connell, who was imprisoned here briefly (and comfortably, thanks to his supporters in Dublin Corporation) in 1844, the Young Irelanders Thomas Francis Meagher and William Smith O'Brien in 1848, and the Fenian leader James Stephens, who escaped from it in 1865 with the aid of replica keys made by warders, who were also members of the IRB, and a number of tables stacked against the wall. It was also the venue for the execution and burial of the Fenian Joseph Poole in 1883; despite later efforts to exhume his remains, they were never found.

In 1892 the prison became a barracks, having been taken over by the War Office, and it fulfilled this role until the 1920s. Renamed Wellington Barracks, it housed a rotating number of British units; the East Surrey Regiment, stationed here in 1914, were part of the British Expeditionary Force despatched to Belgium on the outbreak of the First World War in August 1914. During the Easter Rising Irish Volunteer scouts kept watch on the barracks, though most of the weapons were relocated and it could not have posed any significant threat to the Volunteers in this part of the city. Scouts were sent out from the barracks, and Volunteers in the Jacob's factory on Bishop Street claimed to have been fired upon from it, but it played little role in the Rising, though it was used to house prisoners in the aftermath.

In late 1917 and early 1918 the Dublin Brigade of the IRA obtained weapons from the barracks, either buying them from soldiers or stealing them with the aid of sympathetic soldiers; they used the Grand Canal, which ran behind the barracks between Harold's Cross Bridge and Sally's Bridge, to swim over and back with the guns. In the War of Independence, soldiers from the barracks were ambushed on a number of occasions in its immediate vicinity. It was handed over to the Provisional Government of the Irish Free State in early 1922, and was used as a training depot for soldiers of the new National Army. It also housed military intelligence, led by members of Michael Collins' old 'Squad', and the barracks gained an unenviable reputation for the ill treatment of republican suspects (it was used to hold prisoners from September 1922 onwards). Attacks by the anti-Treaty IRA on both the barracks itself and troops based in it were relatively common during the Civil War. Indeed, on 8 November 1922 members of the anti-Treaty IRA took up positions in buildings behind the barracks, on the southern bank of the Grand Canal, and fired machine guns into the parade ground, killing one soldier and wounding twenty. In reprisal, a number of suspects in the barracks were badly beaten by troops and five were wounded when a soldier fired a machine gun at republican prisoners being held in the gym. The National Army began to patrol Dublin far more intensively in the aftermath of this attack; in that sense, it seems to have been a watershed.

Wellington Barracks was renamed Griffith Barracks in 1923, after Arthur Griffith, and remained in use by the Irish Defence Forces until 1988.

Retrace your steps to Leonard's Corner and turn right, walking up to Harold's Cross bridge across the Grand Canal. On your right will be the stretch of water traversed by IRA Volunteers who stole weapons from the barracks; you can see just how close the canal is to the old barracks complex. Turn left and cross the road, walking along the canal bank away from Harold's Cross bridge. It makes for a pleasant walk, complete with well-fed swans. As you approach Portobello, on the other side of the canal you will the side wall of Cathal Brugha Barracks.

3 | CHURCH OF OUR LADY OF REFUGE, RATHMINES

Turn right at La Touche Bridge at Portobello, and cross the canal into Rathmines. This is one of the old Victorian townships that developed beyond Dublin's canals in the nineteenth century. The township of Rathmines had its own local council, fire service and other amenities prior to independence, and thanks in part to the political affinities of a larger-than-average Protestant community it was decidedly unionist. Indeed, with the exception of Trinity College, in 1918 Rathmines was the only parliamentary constituency outside Ulster to return a unionist MP (Maurice Dockrell) to Westminster. That said, a surprising number of prominent republicans, including Constance Markievicz, also lived in the area.

Even aside from its political complexion, Rathmines was also a relatively wealthy district, as Dublin's middle classes had decamped from the inner city to the newer townships over time. This socio-economic profile was seen to be intertwined with a distinctive accent, which is satirised in Sean O'Casey's 1926 play *The Plough and the Stars*, when a character described as 'a woman from Rathmines' finds herself lost in a tenement during the Easter Rising.

The typical Rathminsian, and even more so the Rathgarian, was a remarkable type. To begin with, he had developed a most peculiar accent which, immediately he opened his mouth, revealed his venue. It is quite impossible to describe the accent in mere words, and it is greatly to be regretted that it disappeared before the coming of recording; a record of it should have been made and preserved in the national archive.

Kevin O'Shiel, Military Archives BMH WS 1770.

Continue up the Rathmines Road and you will pass the Church of Our Lady of Refuge, the enormous dome of which is a major local landmark that can be seen from considerable distances across the city. There is a popular urban myth suggesting that it was originally destined for Russia, before the Bolshevik revolution put paid to any demand for ornate church features there.

Closer to home, the church does have a connection to the Irish revolutionary period. It housed an IRA arms dump in the early phases of the War of Independence, and was also used a place of refuge by IRA members. However, on 26 January 1920, a fire gutted the historic building. This was caused by a switchboard failure and spread rapidly, reaching the dome relatively quickly. Fears that the fire might cause the arms dump to be captured were alleviated by sympathetic members of Dublin Fire Brigade, who assured local members of the IRA that their secret was safe with them.

I told him the true story and asked him to see that the Rathmines people got no inkling whatever of the fact that some dozens of rifles and revolvers were lying in the debris under the floor of the church. He told me not to worry, that nobody would ever know. The incident passed unnoticed by anybody.

> IRA Volunteer Michael Lynch describes talking to Dublin Fire Brigade Chief Officer Captain John Myers, who obviously lent him a sympathetic ear. Military Archives BMH WS 511.

4 PORTOBELLO BARRACKS

Continuing past the church and turning right from Rathmines Road Lower onto Military Road, we approach Cathal Brugha Barracks, originally Portobello Barracks. The barracks is still in use by the Irish Defence Forces and also houses the Military Archives. It is generally closed to the public, but a plaque at the entrance to the barracks honours Francis Sheehy-Skeffington, the writer and activist, who was executed here in dubious circumstances during the Easter Rising. Originally from Cavan, Sheehy-Skeffington attended University College Dublin (UCD) (where he was an associate of James Joyce) and was a prominent teetotaller, vegetarian and pacifist; he was involved with the Irish Citizen Army in its early incarnations, though disagreed with its increasing militarism (he was imprisoned in 1915 for anti-recruiting activities, but was released after going on hunger strike). His dress was apparently distinctive, and was compounded by his refusal to shave (a habit immortalised by Joyce, who nicknamed him 'Hairy Jaysus'). Francis was happy to be described as a crank or, as he put it, 'a small instrument that makes revolutions'. He married Hanna Sheehy, the daughter of the Home Rule MP David Sheehy; the couple took each other's surnames as a gesture of equality.

Leaving his home on the first day of the Rising to try and quell the widespread looting in the city, he was arrested on 25 April on the nearby La Touche Bridge by Captain J.C. Bowen-Colthurst, an Irish-born British Army officer who accused him of being involved in the Rising. During raids in the area, Bowen-Colthurst used Sheehy-Skeffington as a human shield, arresting two journalists (one of whom, Thomas Dickson, had strong unionist political sympathies) and bringing them back to Portobello Barracks as prisoners. All three were shot without trial in the barracks. Bowen-Colthurst was later found guilty but insane for his actions, though he was released relatively soon afterwards.

Sheehy-Skeffington's killing was one of the most notorious instances of British brutality during the Easter Rising. Hanna refused all offers of compensation from the British government and toured the USA from October 1916 to August 1918, speaking at over 250 meetings to bring the injustices of British rule to the attention of the American public; she would remain a notable activist in her own right throughout the revolutionary period and beyond. The plaque was unveiled on 1 April 1970 by Nora Connolly O'Brien, the daughter of James Connolly. During the Civil War, the barracks was the headquarters of the National Army; on 8 January 1922 six anti-Treaty IRA prisoners were executed by firing squad in the barracks.

FRANCIS CHRISTOPHER
SHEEHY SKEFFINGTON
FEMINIST, PACIFIST, SOCIALIST,
REPUBLICAN, SHOT BY FIRING
SQUAD WITHOUT TRIAL IN THIS
BARRACKS ON 26TH APRIL 1916
AGED 37

you whom no power or pride eer awed
whose hand would heal where sharp it fell
smite error on the throne of God
and smile on truth though found in hell
— James Cousins

WALK 2, STOP 4
Commemorative plaque to Francis Sheehy-Skeffington, Portobello Barracks.

5 | PORTOBELLO AND LENNOX STREET

Retrace your steps back to Portobello and cross back into the city over the La Touche Bridge. The pub on the right-hand corner (formerly Davy's, and The Portobello at the time of writing) was another outpost during the Easter Rising, this time for the Irish Citizen Army; it formed the outermost limit of the area seized by the Citizen Army stretching out from St Stephen's Green. Continue on to the corner of Richmond Street and Lennox Street, which is a fitting place to think of 'Little Jerusalem', Dublin's Jewish quarter in the early twentieth century. Dublin's small Jewish community was greatly increased from the 1870s onwards by the arrival of Eastern European migrants who, as either refugees from persecution or as part of the general trend of emigration from the 'Old World', began to settle in Dublin, and soon gravitated to the area between Portobello and Clanbrassil Street, just off the South Circular Road (the Bretzl Bakery opened its doors on Lennox Street in 1870). The size and density of the new community is testified to by the fact that in the 1902 local elections, James Connolly produced his election literature bilingually. To the annoyance of some, this did not mean an Irish translation, but rather a Yiddish one!

Why did this area attract these new arrivals? The quality of the housing is one reason. Walk down Lennox Street today and you will see the distinctive red-brick terraced housing of the Dublin Artisan Dwellings Company, a semi-philanthropic housing body which was coming into its own at the same time the Jewish migrants were arriving in Dublin.

Dublin's Jews soon got involved in politics; some proved to be quite loyalist in their politics, which was understandable as the United Kingdom had given them refuge from persecution, but there was also a Judaeo-Irish Home Rule Association, spearheaded by Jewish businessman Joseph Edelstein, committed to constitutional nationalism. Equally, Jewish radicals in the revolutionary period included Michael Noyk, a lawyer who defended many republicans and who was instrumental in the republican legal system established to undermine British law in Ireland during the War of Independence. Robert Emmet Briscoe, more commonly known as Bob Briscoe, was involved in procuring weapons from the continent for the IRA during the War of Independence, later opposing the Treaty and becoming a founding member of Fianna Fáil and later serving as Lord Mayor of Dublin.

6 CAMDEN STREET

Continue to walk away from Portobello, and straight down Camden Street. Both this and its continuations, Wexford Street and Aungier Street, were originally laid out in the later seventeenth century (indeed, some of the oldest houses in the city are still to be found on Aungier Street). The combined thoroughfare ran from Portobello to Dame Street, which ensured that it was a natural route for troops based in Portobello Barracks. During the War of Independence, the stock in trade of the Dublin IRA was largely a mixture of targeted killings of individuals and ambushes on British forces on the open streets of the city. Camden Street fell into the catchment area of A Company of the 3rd Battalion of the Dublin Brigade and, due to the IRA's use of it as a venue for perhaps a dozen ambushes between December 1920 and

May 1921, it was dubbed the 'Dardanelles' by the British. The bottleneck at Redmond's Hill, the stretch of road between Kevin Street and Aungier Street (just outside the Aungier Street DIT campus) was a particular favourite for ambushes. Grenade attacks on lorries carrying troops became a standard tactic of the IRA, with small-arms fire being used to cover their escape before the weapons were hidden away in dumps.

> *Camden Street, Wexford Street, Redmond's Hill, Aungier Street, George's Street, Dame Street, Parliament Street. This is the area which became known by the British as the "Dardanelles". At Redmond's Hill there was quite a narrow portion of the roadway this became known as the "Narrows". These were all enemy nicknames on the thoroughfares.*

> Joseph O'Connor of the Dublin Brigade of the IRA defines the 'Dardanelles', Military Archives BMH WS 487.

The exchanges of gunfire between British forces and the IRA resulted in civilian as well as military casualties. William Fitzgerald, the three-year-old son of a street trader, was killed by a stray bullet after an ambush outside 17 Camden Street on 6 February 1920, causing the IRA leadership to restrict attacks at busy times such as Saturday evenings. However, two soldiers were killed in a bomb attack on Wexford Street on Saturday 16 March as the area from Kelly's Corner to Wexford Street was being searched by the military.

7 | ROBERT TRESSELL PLAQUE, 37 WEXFORD STREET

Continuing from Camden Street onto Wexford Street, our next stop is associated with a revolutionary writer more widely known abroad than at home today. A plaque high on 37 Wexford Street honours Robert Noonan (1870–1911), better known by his penname, Robert Tressell. The son of an RIC officer, he came to international prominence after his death with the

WALK 2, STOP 7 ■

*Commemorative plaque to Robert Tressell,
socialist author and leading participant
in 1898 centenary in the Transvaal.*

publication of *The Ragged-Trousered Philanthropists*, a classic of working-class and socialist literature. His Dublin plaque includes a hammer and a paintbrush.

Noonan was in South Africa for the centenary of the United Irish rebellion of 1798, and involved himself in commemorations there with Arthur Griffith, John MacBride and other Irishmen in the Transvaal. Though he assisted in the foundation of the Irish Brigade which fought on the side of the Boers, he does not seem to have actively participated in the fighting himself, departing for Britain as the conflict began.

The Ragged-Trousered Philanthropists is often overlooked, and tells the story of Frank Owen, a travelling socialist organiser wishing to inject class radicalism into English workers. To Owen, 'The present system – competition – capitalism … it's no good tinkering at it. Everything about it is wrong and there's nothing about it that's right. There's only one thing to be done with it and that is to smash it up and have a different system altogether.'

Tressell died of tuberculosis in Liverpool in 1911.

8 JACOB'S FACTORY

Continue north along Wexford Street until you reach the junction of Bishop Street; turn left here to find the location of the old Jacob's factory. This huge installation occupied a block in this area and was another of the outposts seized during the Easter Rising. The biscuit-making firm of W. & R. Jacob's was one the largest employers in early twentieth-century Dublin after Guinness. Jacob's had locked out ITGWU members in September 1913, and had been notably slow to readmit them to employment afterwards (and even then had forced them to submit to humiliating medical examinations). Figures such as James Connolly and Delia Larkin had condemned it for its anti-union stance, and the poor treatment of its workers. The firm was later criticised by Connolly for allegedly encouraging, or at least facilitating, recruitment during the First World War.

The factory was seized on Easter Monday, 24 April 1916, by perhaps 100 members of the 2nd Battalion of the Dublin Brigade of the Irish Volunteers

under Thomas MacDonagh. The factory itself was an enormous and formidable Victorian edifice located on the 'block' enclosed by Bishop Street, Bride Street, Peter's Street and Peter's Row, and between St Patrick's

■ **WALK 2, STOP 8**

A contemporary image of Jacob's factory on Bishop Street.
(Courtesy of Dublin City Library and Archives)

Cathedral and St Stephen's Green. Its seizure helped to complete a loop of buildings across the south inner city. The factory had two large towers that could act as observation points, while its location was very close to both Camden Street and Patrick Street, natural routes for troops entering the city centre from Portobello Barracks in Rathmines and Wellington Barracks on the South

Circular Road. There were only a few staff present in the building when the Volunteers broke into it; a number of smaller outposts were established in the area around the factory.

Troops coming from Portobello and Wellington Barracks could easily bypass it and so, though it was fired upon from nearby Dublin Castle, Jacob's saw relatively little action. While the garrison saw some fighting early in the week, their principal enemies proved to be boredom and the locals: the factory was surrounded by tenements, and the Volunteers were attacked and abused by residents, many of whom were Jacob's workers themselves. The families of servicemen (of whom there were many in this area) were also quite hostile, but there may have been another reason for this hostility: Michael O'Hanrahan, who was in Jacob's, expressed his concern that the choice of location might endanger local residents if the British chose to attack.

> *We inspected a barricade at the head of Fumbally Lane and I*
> *parted then with Dick McKee – I forget exactly when. We took*
> *several police and plain-clothes men prisoners, and I was in*
> *charge of them for a while. Jack Twomey was with me and we*
> *brought our prisoners back to Jacobs when it [was] getting*
> *dusk in the evening. The women around the Coombe were*
> *in a terrible state, they were like French revolution furies*
> *and were throwing their arms round the police, hugging and*
> *kissing them, much to the disgust of the police.*
> *I got a few kicks and I think Twomey got some too,*
> *but somebody fired a shot to clear them off and they*
> *went away.*

Thomas Pugh, Military Archives BMH WS 397.

MacDonagh surrendered in nearby St Patrick's Park on Sunday 30 April; some of the factory was looted after the Volunteers had left. Three members of the Jacob's garrison were executed for their role in the Rising: Michael

O'Hanrahan, Thomas MacDonagh and John MacBride. The latter, who was a veteran of the Boer War, apparently beseeched his fellow volunteers never to let themselves be cooped up in a building again. Most of the factory was eventually demolished, though fragments of the ground storey and one of the towers are still visible on Bishop Street between the DIT campus on Aungier Street and the National Archives of Ireland.

9 | DUBLIN CASTLE

Walk to the end of Bishop Street and turn right down Bride Street. Across the road is St Patrick's Park, from where British troops machine-gunned Marsh's Library; the corner of the park nearest Bishop Street is where Thomas MacDonagh surrendered at the end of the Easter Rising. Continue past the red-brick Victorian Iveagh Trust buildings (built at the turn of the century for Guinness employees and their families) until you get to Ship Street (the name is a bastardised version of 'Sheep' Street, harking back to when it housed a medieval livestock market). This is the back entrance to Dublin Castle, and would have been used by troops sent to reinforce the castle garrison during the Easter Rising; immediately to the right of the gate is the old Ship Street Barracks, which housed the castle garrison and which was used to detain prisoners temporarily during the Easter Rising.

Dublin Castle was also targeted by militant suffragettes. In June 1912, members of the Irish Womens' Franchise League (IWFL), including leading activist Hanna Sheehy-Skeffington, smashed a number of the castle's windows at the Ship Street entrance. A number of the activists were charged and sentenced to one month's hard labour. Sheehy-Skeffinton recalled how 'the policeman who grabbed my arm instinctively seized the right, and as I am left-handed, that gave me a chance to get in a few more panes before the military arrived and my escort led me off.' Marjorie Hasler, another IWFL activist imprisoned in 1912, would insist that 'we don't like smashing glass any more than men like smashing skulls. Yet in both cases there is, I believe, a strong feeling that something must be broken before a wrong is changed into a right.' Out of the window-smashing frenzy came a wonderful street rhyme:

Mary had a little bag, and in it was a hammer.
For Mary was a Suffragette for votes she used to clamour.
She broke a pane of glass one day, like any naughty boy.
A constable he came along, and now she's in Mountjoy

Continue through the castle itself, turning left around the Chapel Royal and through the lower castle yard to reach the upper castle yard. Dublin Castle dates back to the Middle Ages, though most of the buildings that the complex consists of are eighteenth- and nineteenth-century constructions. For some nationalists and republicans, Dublin Castle was viewed in a manner akin to Mordor in Tolkien's novel *The Lord of the Rings*; as the centre of British rule in Ireland from the thirteenth century up until the British withdrawal in 1922, it was the font of all evil. Its symbolic value to opponents of British rule was undeniable yet, oddly enough, it survived the revolution unscathed.

On the first day of the Easter Rising, the Irish Citizen Army under the command of Seán Connolly arrived at the Cork Hill gates of the castle. Constable James O'Brien was shot here, with Helena Molony recalling that 'When Connolly went to get past him, the Sergeant *[sic]* put out his arm and Connolly shot him dead.' Members of the Citizen Army entered the gates and briefly took control of the neighbouring guardroom. The gunfire at the gate drew the attention of officers attending a meeting that was taking place within the complex and one ran across the courtyard discharging his pistol (ironically, as this was a public holiday, most of the castle garrison had the day off).

The castle withstood the Rising and continued to house the British administration in Ireland throughout the revolutionary period. It also hosted the transfer of power in January 1922 when the last viceroy, Lord Fitzallen, handed over power to the new Provisional Government of the Irish Free State in the form of Michael Collins. *The Irish Times* noted the following day that 'having withstood the attacks of successive generations of rebels, it was quietly handed over yesterday to eight gentlemen in three taxicabs.'

Commemorative mural of the Battle of Clontarf, City Hall.
(Courtesy Paul Reynolds)

10 CITY HALL

Leaving the upper castle yard through the arched gate beside the Bedford Tower, you will find Dublin City Hall to your immediate right. The elegant Georgian City Hall, located at the intersection of Parliament Street and Dame Street, was originally opened as the Royal Exchange in the 1770s and was reopened as the city hall in 1852. It is another of the buildings occupied during the Easter Rising and a building that played other roles during the revolutionary period. The front and sides of the building are pockmarked with small-arms fire, though it is unclear precisely whether this was from 1916 or later during the Civil War of 1922. It was the scene of the first engagement of the Easter Rising. On the afternoon 24 April members of the Irish Citizen Army led by Seán Connolly, who worked in the Motor Tax Office in City Hall, and who may have been the model for Jack Clitheroe in Seán O'Casey's play *The Plough and the Stars* (O'Casey had been acquainted with him).

■ **WALK 5, STOP 10**

*Commemorative
plaque to Seán
Connolly, City Hall.
(Courtesy Las Fallon)*

WALK 2, STOP 10 ■
Mosaic of Dublin city's coat of arms, City Hall.
(Courtesy Las Fallon)

The Citizen Army managed to enter City Hall with a minimum of fuss, as Connolly apparently had the keys. Having killed the first victim of the Rising, in one of history's ironies Connolly himself seems to have been the first insurgent victim of the Rising, when, at around 2pm, he was shot in the stomach while on the roof of City Hall. Had the Rising not gone ahead, he was to have appeared on stage that night in a performance of W.B. Yeats' *Cathleen Ni Houlihan.* He is buried in Glasnevin Cemetery and a plaque at the front of the building commemorates him and the other insurgents killed at City Hall.

There was a logic to the seizure of City Hall. Given that it overlooks the upper castle gate, it was the perfect place to ambush troops coming out of Dublin Castle. Other buildings in the area were seized and this happened in other districts as well. The insurgents would seize a large building such as City Hall and install outposts in other nearby buildings, in this case, in the buildings on both corners of Parliament Street, directly across from it. The garrison in Dublin Castle was immediately reinforced when the Rising broke out, and heavy fighting took place in the vicinity of City Hall until troops broke into the building later that day and overwhelmed the small garrison; the building itself suffered only minor damage. The fact that it was only seized for a few hours, however, is useful in one sense because the building avoided the devastation visited upon some other buildings, such as the GPO. A second, much newer, memorial plaque on the exterior commemorates and names all members of the small Citizen Army garrison.

The presence of women in the ranks of the Citizen Army surprised the British soldiers who eventually overcame the garrison here.

> *It would never occur to them, of course, that they were women soldiers. Actually, the women in the Citizen Army were not first-aiders, but did military work, except where it suited them to be first-aiders. Even before the Russian Army had women soldiers, the Citizen Army had them. The British officers thought these girls had been taken prisoner by the rebels. They asked them: "Did they do anything to you? Were they kind to you? how many are up here?" Jinny Shanahan – quick enough – answered: "No, they did not do anything to us. There are hundreds upstairs – big guns and everything."*

Helena Molony, Military Archives BMH WS 391.

City Hall played numerous roles throughout the revolutionary period. The funerals of Thomas Ashe, Arthur Griffith and Michael Collins all began from City Hall before making their circuitous route through Dublin towards Glasnevin Cemetery on the north of the city. In December 1920 it was eventually requisitioned for military purposes by the British authorities, partly as they had grown weary of the political stance of the republican-dominated city council, which met in the building. In early 1922 City Hall briefly housed the first Free State Government as it took over power from the outgoing British administration, which led Free State Minister Kevin O'Higgins to quip that the provisional government consisted of a number of men standing amid the ruins of one administration in City Hall 'with wild men screaming through the keyhole'.

Inside the building, the impressive rotunda contains a mosaic featuring Dublin's coat of arms, installed in 1898 to a design by City Architect C.J. McCarthy. The motto of the city, *'Obedientia Civium Urbis Felicitas'*, roughly translates as 'The obedience of the citizens produces a happy city.' It is perhaps out of sync with the revolutionary heritage of Dublin in this era. The murals around the rotunda were painted between 1913 and 1919, and depict various scenes from the history of the city, such as the arrival of the Vikings and the prelude to the Battle of Clontarf in 1014, when the forces of the high king Brian Boru defeated a coalition spearheaded by the Vikings of Dublin. The emphasis on foreign invaders and Irish victories over them indicates a nationalistic undertone characteristic of the cultural activism of this era.

Finally, look between the legs of the statue of the eighteenth-century alderman Charles Lucas; a bullet seems to have pierced his cloak.

11 | BLOODY SUNDAY PLAQUE, EXCHANGE COURT

Exit City Hall by the front entrance and turn right to Exchange Court, now an open plaza, but at this time the headquarters of Dublin Metropolitan Police's 'G' Division, with responsibility for political policing. In the corner closest to City Hall there is also a plaque to one of the lesser-known events of Bloody Sunday in November 1920: the extrajudicial killings by British forces of Peadar Clancy, Conor Clune and Dick McKee in this building. McKee and Clancy were senior members of the IRA, detained in a raid the night before. Clune was an innocent civilian, who was simply in the wrong place at the wrong time.

WALK 2, STOP 11
*Commemorative
plaque to Bloody
Sunday deaths,
Exchange Court.*

Interestingly, the memorial replaced the royal insignia that was destroyed in a bomb attack on 11 November 1937. Cross the open plaza to the post box on Palace Street, the street that leads directly to the lower castle gate. James Connolly said that Irish independence would be meaningless if the change it brought was no more meaningful than painting pillar boxes green. This pre-1922 pillar box still retains the royal insignia, and was apparently the first of its kind in the city to be painted green.

Cross Dame Street. Turn right and then left into Eustace Street.

12 QUAKER MEETING HOUSE AND PLAQUE TO UNITED IRISHMEN

On Eustace Street, a plaque on the Society of Friends' building honours the Society of United Irishmen, whose Dublin branch was established at a meeting here, in a tavern called The Eagle, in November 1791. The United Irishmen began life as a political club which wished to bring about parliamentary reform. Within a few short years, it was a revolutionary republican force, driven underground after the outbreak of war between France and Britain. Taking Thomas Paine's *The Rights of Man* as their core political text (it remains the most influential and best-selling political pamphlet in Irish history, and was declared 'the Koran of Belfast' by Theobald Wolfe Tone), the society established fraternal links with radical societies in England and with the French Directory, which sent military assistance to Ireland to support a United Irish insurrection. The rebellion of 1798 was a military failure, but was also a major milestone in the birth of separatist republicanism. For many participants in the Irish revolutionary period, the centenary of the 1798 Rebellion was a catalyst in their own political development and consciousness. In Ireland, America, Australia and even in the mining towns of South Africa, Irish separatists seized upon historical commemoration as a means of drumming up support for Irish separatism. To James Connolly, the radicals of the revolutionary period followed in the footsteps of the United Irishmen, as 'Wolfe Tone was abreast of the revolutionary thought of his day, as are the Socialist Republicans of our day'. The plaque may not have a direct link with the Irish revolution but it indicates a fundamental part of the genealogy of that revolution.

To join up with the third walk, return to Dame Street and turn left, walking until you reach the Bank of Ireland on College Green.

WALK 2, STOP12 ■

The seal of the Society of United Irishmen, founded in 1791.

WALK 3

THE SOUTH-EAST INNER CITY

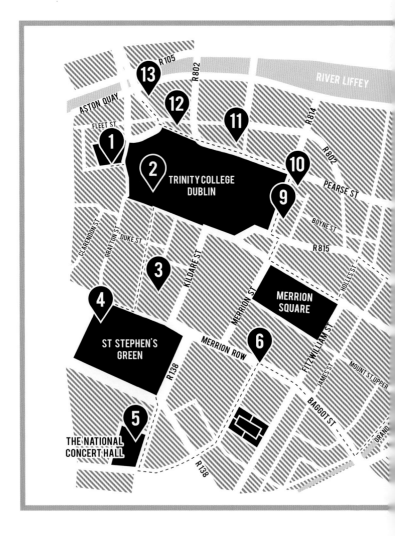

Introduction

This is the second of the two walks through Dublin's south inner city, and takes the form of an elongated loop that begins in College Green and extends out to the Grand Canal before returning back to the vicinity of Trinity College. This takes in some of the finer Georgian architecture of the city, and also some the scenes of some of the heaviest fighting of the Easter Rising. It was also the location of some of the best-known events of the War of Independence and one of the most notorious of the Civil War.

1. COLLEGE GREEN

2. TRINITY COLLEGE DUBLIN

3. THE MANSION HOUSE

4. ST STEPHEN'S GREEN AND ROYAL COLLEGE OF SURGEONS

5. EARLSFORT TERRACE

6. BAGGOT STREET

7. MOUNT STREET

8. BOLAND'S MILLS

9. ORIEL HOUSE

10. WESTLAND ROW

11. PEARSE FAMILY BUSINESS

12. PEARSE STREET GARDA STATION

13. FENIAN OFFICES, D'OLIER STREET

1 COLLEGE GREEN

College Green, originally known as Hoggen Green, once lay outside the boundaries of medieval Dublin. The city grew around it. It began to be laid out in its current form from the 1680s. By the 1730s, it had acquired the building that arguably defines it: the neoclassical Parliament House, now the Bank of Ireland, which from 1731 until 1800 housed Ireland's semi-autonomous (and exclusively male and Protestant) parliament. From 1801, Ireland became part of the United Kingdom of Great Britain and Ireland, and the injustice and misgovernment that was seen to be the legacy of the union was an ongoing source of resentment. All shades of Irish nationalists agreed that British rule was a bad thing; where they disagreed was on the alternative. The Parliament House, in relation to the revolutionary era, symbolises the promise of Home Rule. Prior to the Easter Rising in 1916, Home Rule was the dominant ideology for nationalist Ireland, and the assumption was that this modest measure of autonomy would result in a parliament that would reoccupy the old eighteenth-century parliament building. The building had enormous symbolism for nationalists in the nineteenth and early twentieth centuries on this basis. While John Redmond's Irish Parliamentary Party (IPP) had managed to extract a Home Rule bill from the British Liberal government in 1914 (subject to avoiding an Ulster Unionist rebellion), it was suspended on the outbreak of the First World War. By the time the war had ended, Redmond was dead and events had overtaken his party. It never became the parliament of an independent Ireland; the cost of compensating the Bank of Ireland for the loss of what was then its headquarters would have been prohibitive.

You can see a symbolic protest against British rule in College Green: while the royal crest is still visible above the portico of the Bank of Ireland, directly across College Green on the Old National Bank is a statue of Hibernia, apparently placed there in the 1890s and carved by James Pearse, the father of Patrick Pearse, a symbolic challenge, one might say, to the royal authority on the other side of College Green.

College Green hosted a range of public gatherings in this era, from the official parade marking the end of the First World War in July 1919 to pro-Treaty rallies in early 1922. Before leaving it behind, it is worth noting something that is no longer there: Grinling Gibbons' equestrian statue of William III (William of Orange) in Roman garb (complete with laurel wreath). Erected in 1701, it was targeted by numerous groups over the centuries and was removed after it was bombed on the morning of Armistice Day, 11 November 1928, in one of a series of co-ordinated attacks on what were presumably deemed to be symbols of British imperialism in Dublin (the other monumental victims were a statue of George II in St Stephen's Green and a memorial fountain to Edward VII in Herbert Park). The explosion blew out most of the windows on College Green. As for the statue itself, it lost some of the left hind leg and a portion of the pedestal on which it rested: not enough to destroy it, but enough for it to be rendered unstable (the Gardaí, who had exchanged gunfire with those who planted the bomb, were apparently glad to be rid of it; they had long deemed the statue to be a traffic nuisance). Due to its association with the British military, Armistice Day was a contentious date in the 1920s, and while the revolution may have ended in 1923, it continued to have an afterlife on the streets thereafter. College Green in the early 1920s was a common and popular venue for massive Armistice Day commemorations of the Irish dead of the First World War.

On the other side of College Green, across from the bank, is the west front of Trinity College Dublin. Make your way across College Green and enter the front gate.

2 TRINITY COLLEGE DUBLIN

Trinity College was founded in 1592 and was extensively reconstructed in the eighteenth and nineteenth centuries (the west front facing onto College Green is arguably the most imposing piece of Georgian architecture in Dublin). Until 1793, entrance to Trinity was restricted to members of the Church of Ireland, and at the start of the twentieth century the student body and staff would still have been overwhelmingly Protestant (mainly Church of Ireland), and broadly, though not exclusively, unionist in outlook. One of Trinity's sitting MPs throughout this period was, after all, the Dublin-born Unionist leader, Edward Carson (who was born on Harcourt Street). Although

Carson was associated with Ulster Unionism, Dublin had a significant Unionist population for whom Trinity College was a key institution.

Entering the front gate you pass under Regent House, which in 1917–18 was the venue for the 'Irish Convention', a conference that was intended to explore common ground between unionists and nationalists to allow for the introduction of Home Rule, though as this was boycotted by Ulster Unionists and Sinn Féin, nothing came of it.

Trinity played a significant role in the Easter Rising. When the Rising began on 24 April, the porters closed the gates and implored any troops in uniform on the streets to help the college's Officer Training Corps (OTC) to defend the campus. A motley assortment of over 40 troops, including ANZAC (Australian and New Zealand Army Corps) and South African troops on leave in Dublin, found themselves manning positions in and around Parliament (Front) Square, and occupying positions on the roof of the West Front, which enabled them to act as snipers; a republican messenger, Gerald Keogh, was shot dead outside the college and his body was left in the Provost's House for a number of days before being buried briefly on the playing fields on the east of the campus.

■ **WALK 3, STOP 2**
Trinity College Dublin.
(Courtesy Dennis Horgan)

The upper windows were strongly barricaded, and machine guns were placed in positions on the parapet, while snipers took up favourable positions on the roof. Dawn had scarcely appeared when the effect of these precautions was demonstrated. Rebel scouts on bicycles rushed up Dame Street in an attempt to get in touch with St Stephen's Green, where the rebels were ensconced. The leaders, however, had scarcely turned the corner of Grafton Street when they were laid low by well-directed shots by two colonial sharpshooters. The others scattered pell-mell up the side streets.

The Irish Times *describes the firing from the nearby West Front of Trinity College, from* The Sinn Fein Rebellion Handbook *(Dublin, 1917).*

The 'houses' in Parliament Square are numbered. House 15 acted as a medical station during the Rising. Trinity's central location proved advantageous to the British, and by Wednesday 26 April members of the Leinster Regiment began to occupy the campus, which ultimately housed as many as 4,000 troops during the Rising. Oddly enough, some students turned up for exams on 25 and 26 April, before the fighting in the city became too intense.

Continuing into the centre of Parliament Square, you will see a squat, octagonal building to the right. The 1937 Reading Room is a rare example of an Irish memorial to the Great War, a contentious issue that overlapped with the struggle for independence. Over 3,000 graduates, students and staff of the college enlisted, and the reading room commemorates the 471 students and staff and alumni of the university killed during the First World War; the names are listed inside the entrance hall, which is not open to the public and was opened as a stand-alone structure in 1929. The reading room itself was opened by Éamon de Valera in 1937.

The campus has one memorial to a victim of the Easter Rising. Go around the 1937 Reading Room into Fellows' Square and turn left, continuing past the Old Library and the newer modernist Berkeley Library until you reach the cricket pitch. Turn left and continue to the car park; along the main wall at Nassau Street, near the end of the path, there is a memorial plaque to Private Arthur Charles Smith of the 4th Hussars, killed in the Rising on 29 April; he was briefly buried in this very spot and the original plaque was erected by the Trinity College OTC. The cricket pitch itself was the venue for an IRA attack on 3 June 1921, when a cricket match between the 'gentlemen of Ireland' and the 'military of Ireland' was fired upon from the railings at Kildare Street. A 21-year-old medical student, Kathleen Wright, was killed; the attackers were never caught.

After 1922, Trinity College regularly continued to fly the Union Flag and 'God Save the King' remained the national anthem as far as many in the college were concerned throughout the 1920s.

Return to Fellows' Square via the plaza located between the Berkeley and Ussher libraries. Follow the path alongside the Arts Building and exit Trinity by the ramp located at the end, which will direct you to the Nassau Street gate to the college.

3 THE MANSION HOUSE

Leaving Trinity College via its Nassau Street side entrance, cross to Dawson Street, which is directly opposite the entrance. Continue along the left side of the street until you come to a small plaza at which an old townhouse is set back. This is the Mansion House, the official residence of the Lord Mayor of Dublin since 1715 and one of the most important sites of the Irish revolution. Built for the property developer Joshua Dawson in 1710, it was sold to Dublin Corporation in May 1715. The position of Lord Mayor has been occupied by constitutional nationalists (like Daniel O'Connell), unionists (Sir Benjamin Lee Guinness) and republicans, including Kathleen Clarke, the first female Lord Mayor of Dublin and the widow of 1916 leader Thomas J. Clarke. The city coat of arms appears over the building, as it does on municipal buildings across the city.

Architecturally, it is one of the most impressive eighteenth-century homes in Dublin, but there are a few more recent additions that should be pointed out. Note the cast-iron canopy over the entrance, erected in 1900 in anticipation of the royal visit of Queen Victoria, who was denounced by nationalist protestors as the 'Famine Queen'. An increasingly nationalistic Dublin Corporation offered no official welcome on the occasion of royal visits like that in 1903, and the 1911 royal visit proved particularly controversial, with protests in the city organised by Seán Mac Diarmada, James Connolly and others.

The Mansion House was the venue for a number of important gatherings throughout the revolutionary period. On 25 September 1914 the streets around Dawson Street were closed off by the DMP as Prime Minister Herbert Asquith and John Redmond both addressed a packed meeting in the Mansion House, imploring Irishmen (including the majority of the Irish Volunteers who had remained loyal to Redmond) to enlist in the British Army during the war; the security cordon was due to concerns about a counter-demonstration organised by the ITGWU. In October 1917 Sinn Féin held its first significant gatherings since the Easter Rising in the Mansion House, and elected Éamon de Valera to its leadership. This signified the reorganisation of Arthur Griffith's Sinn Féin party into a more radical form. Sinn Féin adopted a commitment 'to securing the international recognition of Ireland as an independent Irish Republic' at

RUSSIAN REPUBLIC RECEPTION.

❧ MASS ❧
MEETING
. IN .
Round Room, Mansion House,
. ON .
MONDAY, FEBRUARY 4th,
AT 8 P.M.   *1918*

To Congratulate the Russian People on the triumph they
have won for Democratic Principles.

SPEAKERS :

Mr. Wm. O'Brien	Mr. Cathal O'Shannon
Mr. L. Ginnell	Mrs. Connery
Madame Markievicz	Mr. P. Coates
Mr. Thomas Foran	Mr J. J. Hughes
Madame Gonne-McBride	And Russian Bolsheviks

RUSSIA RECOGNISES IRELAND.

IRELAND ! RESPOND TO RUSSIA !

WALK 3, STOP 3 ■
A poster advertising a meeting in sympathy with the Russian Revolution, February 1918.

the Mansion House, a far cry from the more moderate demands of Griffith's party before 1916.

In February 1918, a crowd estimated to be in the region of 10,000 gathered here for a meeting to herald the Soviet revolution, spilling into the neighbouring streets. Speakers including Constance Markievicz, trade union leader William O'Brien and the Riga-born radical Konrad Peterson addressed the gathered masses, and newspapers reported that a red flag flew alongside the tricolour. While there would be more than 100 so-called 'Soviets' throughout Ireland during the War of Independence, the enthusiasm shown for the Bolsheviks at the Mansion House gathering quickly waned.

> *The scene in the Round Room was an extraordinary one. The passage up the centre of the spacious and crowded floor was occupied by a dense body of men standing. Near the front of this body was borne aloft a red flag, and during an interval in proceedings, while a collection was being taken up, the song "The Red Flag" was sung.*

> The Irish Independent *of 5 February 1918 describes a pro-Bolshevik meeting.*

Most significantly, the Mansion House is synonymous with the first Dáil, which met here in January 1919 following Sinn Féin's resounding victory in the 1918 general election, the first to be held since the outbreak of the World War. Standing on an abstentionist platform, the party secured 73 seats from a possible 105, at the expense of the IPP. Refusing to sit in Westminster, Sinn Féin's parliamentarians (those not imprisoned or on the run) met in the Round Room of the Mansion House on 21 January 1919; the day is also taken as the starting date of the Irish War of Independence, after an ambush at Soloheadbeg in Tipperary led by the IRA fighters Dan Breen and Sean Treacy. Ironically, the Mansion House had hosted a reception for veterans of the Royal Dublin Fusiliers earlier that day.

At the first meeting of the Dáil, a Democratic Programme was read, which declared that 'we desire our country to be ruled in accordance with the principles of Liberty, Equality, and Justice for all, which alone can secure permanence of Government in the willing adhesion of the people.' The Dáil was viewed as an illegitimate assembly by Westminster, and was thus declared illegal in April 1919.

The Mansion House continued to host public and political meetings of various kinds throughout the revolutionary period. A particularly striking one was a rally of ex-servicemen in July 1919 under the banner of the 'Irish Nationalist Veterans Association', who protested against the British treatment of First World War veterans such as themselves, while also stating that they would boycott the official victory parade marking the end of the war in protest at what they described as 'the coercion of this country'.

ST STEPHENS GREEN AND ROYAL COLLEGE OF SURGEONS

Continue along to the end of Dawson Street, and you come to St Stephen's Green, originally laid out in the 1660s, but redeveloped in the 1870s. It was a natural junction that commanded the approaches to a large tract of the south-east inner city. Turn right and head for the main entrance, which is marked by a large arch. This is Fusiliers' Arch, erected in 1907 to commemorate members of the Royal Dublin Fusiliers who were killed in the Boer War at the turn of the twentieth century. The Dublin Fusiliers were the main unit to recruit from Dublin city and, because of Dublin's chronic lack of opportunity for unskilled labour, joining the colours was by no means unusual. The names of the dead are inscribed inside the arch, on the ceiling. On the other hand, a relatively

WALK 3, STOP 4 ■
St Stephen's Green.
(Courtesy Dennis Horgan)

■ **WALK 3, STOP 4**
Above and right: Battle damage on the facade of the Royal College of Surgeons.

Far right: Battle damage from 1916 on Fusiliers' Arch at the main entrance to St Stephen's Green. (Courtesy Las Fallon)

small band of Irish nationalists, under the command of Irish-American military leader John Blake and Westport native John MacBride, fought alongside the Boers in opposition to what they saw as British colonial aggression in the Transvaal. On the other side of the conflict, about 28,000 Irishmen fought within the ranks of the British Army during the war; on at least one occasion, these two very different bands of Irishmen found themselves in direct conflict in the Transvaal. Nonetheless, the struggle of Boer settlers against the British captured the sympathy of many Irish nationalists of all stripes, with figures such as James Connolly and Arthur Griffith (who had lived in South Africa for a period) being vocal sympathisers with the Boer cause.

On the other hand, St Stephen's Green was supposed to be the venue for a republican memorial that was never completed. Elaborate ceremonials accompanied the laying of the foundation stone on 15 August 1898 ('Wolfe Tone Day'). The stone was quarried from Cave Hill outside Belfast (where the United Irishmen had been founded) and inscribed with '1798. Tribute to Theobald Wolfe Tone, patriot. Belfast nationalists '98 centenary association'; it proved impossible to erect it in Belfast, so it was sent by train to Dublin where it took pride of place at the head of an elaborate ceremonial procession, attended by what one observer put at

100,000 people, with 80 bands, banners and decorative arches, and even a green flag hanging off Nelson's Pillar. The procession began at Parnell Square and went west, stopping at various locations associated with 1798 until it reached St Stephen's Green, where the veteran Fenian John O'Leary dedicated it, drawing explicit links to the republican tradition and laying the stone into place with a trowel donated by Tone's American granddaughter. Six taps signified the four provinces, France (symbolising the United Irishmen) and the US (symbolising the Fenians). The location was deliberately chosen in what was perceived as a unionist district. This was about more that just putting up a statue; the fact that it was never erected perhaps proves the point. Such ceremonies, and indeed the campaign against the Boer War, helped to revive 'advanced' nationalism at the turn of the century, and can be seen as a prelude to the revolutionary period. At the same time, the failure to get enough public subscriptions to erect the monument is in stark contrast to the fact that Fusiliers' Arch (often dubbed, uncharitably, 'Traitors' Gate') actually was erected.

If you look up at the eastern edge of the memorial arch, you can see that it is scarred by machine-gun fire, a legacy of the Easter Rising. On 24 April 1916, members of the Irish Citizen Army led by Michael Mallin (a former British Army veteran) seized St Stephen's Green. The Citizen Army were met with considerable hostility as they ejected civilians from the park, which was magnified into outrage after a civilian was shot while trying to retrieve a vehicle from a barricade they had erected near the Shelbourne Hotel. Within the park itself, trenches were dug, seemingly near the gates of the park, as the Citizen Army sought to fortify their positions, though their exact location is unclear. In the early hours of Tuesday morning, the troops that had been sent to the district began to attack the Citizen Army positions in the park. The Shelbourne Hotel provided a natural vantage point overlooking the park, and troops were able to fire down into the trenches that had been dug. Within a matter of hours Mallin and those under his command were forced to abandon the green and they retreated to the Royal College of Surgeons. As British attention shifted elsewhere, the fighting eased off. Mallin and his garrison surrendered the following Sunday. The Royal College of Surgeons building is on the west side of the green, near the Luas track, and the marks of gunfire can be seen across its façade as well.

> As I drew near the Green rifle fire began like sharply-cracking
> whips. It was from the further side. I saw that the Gates were
> closed and men were standing inside with guns on their shoul-
> ders. I passed a house, the windows of which were smashed in.
> As I went by a man in civilian clothes slipped through the Park
> gates, which instantly closed behind him. He ran towards me,
> and I halted ... In the centre of this side of the Park a rough bar-
> ricade of carts and motor cars had been sketched. It was still full
> of gaps. Behind it was a halted tram, and along the vistas of the
> Green one saw other trams derelict, untenanted.

> The journalist James Stephens describes the beginning of the Rising at
> St Stephen's Green, from his book The Insurrection in Dublin (Dublin,
> 1917).

Enter the park itself, bearing in mind that the opening times vary throughout the year. A small detour south following the Luas line will bring you to Harcourt Street, where number 6, near the St Stephen's Green end, was the headquarters of Sinn Féin throughout the revolutionary period; Michael Collins retained his finance offices here throughout the War of Independence, when it was regularly raided.

Re-enter the green and walk towards its central plaza. There are numerous memorials scattered throughout the park; the events of 1916 are represented by a bust of Constance Markievicz, who held a senior role in the Citizen Army garrison that had tried to occupy the park. On the east side of the plaza is one of the more striking memorials in the park: the bust of Thomas Kettle, erected in 1927 and which states, enigmatically, that he was killed at Guincy in 1916. This is due to objections to the original inscription, for Kettle was killed in the course of the Battle of the Somme whilst serving in the British Army. Kettle was born in Artane, County Dublin, into a prominent and wealthy family with strong links to the Home Rule movement. In July 1906 he was elected MP for East Tyrone. Kettle was liberal on many social issues (such as women's suffrage), with a notably cosmopolitan outlook that later influenced his views on the First World War.

In 1909 he married Mary Sheehy (daughter of the nationalist MP David Sheehy, and the sister-in-law of Francis Sheehy-Skeffington), and Kettle's personal and political connections helped him obtain the post of professor of national economics at UCD. On the outbreak of the First World War he was in Belgium purchasing weapons for the Irish Volunteers. Kettle took the view that the struggle against Germany transcended Anglo-Irish politics and he supported John Redmond's stance on the war. He was, however, unable to obtain a front-line commission owing to ill-health caused by alcoholism, and was instead commissioned as a recruiting officer. In this capacity he proved a combative advocate of the war effort, and came into open conflict with advanced nationalists opposed to Redmondite support for the war. However, Kettle could not avoid criticism that he was seeking recruits for a war in which he was unable to fight himself. This was an issue that troubled him deeply, and after numerous attempts he was finally sent to the Western Front with the Royal Dublin Fusiliers. Ironically, by this time he had become deeply disillusioned with the war. He acerbically noted of the executed leaders of the Rising (some of whom he knew personally) that 'these men will go down in history as heroes and martyrs; and I will go down – if I go down at all – as a bloody British officer'. He chose to remain at the front, where he was a popular officer amongst his men. Kettle was killed at Guincy, during the Somme offensive, on 9 September 1916. The memorial incorporates a stanza from his most famous poem, 'To my daughter Betty', written while he was at the front; it can be taken as his political testament.

A statue of King George II, erected in 1756 on an extremely tall pedestal in the centre of the park that was intended to guarantee its visibility, was destroyed by explosion on morning of 13 May 1937, the day after the coronation of George VI.

Continue through St Stephen's Green until you reach the south-east corner, and cross the road to Earlsfort Terrace.

WALK 3, STOP 5 ■
Detail from the gates of the
National Concert Hall
on Earlsfort Terrace.

5   EARLSFORT TERRACE

E arlsfort Terrace, off the south-east corner of St Stephen's Green, is home to the National Concert Hall. The limestone-fronted building was originally constructed for the Dublin International Exhibition of Arts and Manufactures of 1865, later becoming the central building of the National University of Ireland (later University College Dublin). Some prominent participants in the revolutionary period worked and studied in the National University, including Thomas MacDonagh and Eoin MacNeill. Agnes O'Farrelly, a lecturer of the university, was a founding member of Cumann na mBan. During the War of Independence, Frank Flood and Kevin Barry, two students of the university, were hanged in Mountjoy Prison.

I came up to a Dublin still smoking from Easter Week. The first European war was still on, and all general conditions were sad and miserable. We were a hungry, untidy, dirty lot – we of 1917– 19 … There was of course, unceasing political and patriotic argument, as at the time was inevitable. There was also good theatre.

The novelist Kate O'Brien recalls student life in UCD in 1917–19, University Review *(Autumn 1955).*

The National University building on Earlsfort Terrace was also the venue for many of the Dáil Éireann debates on the Anglo-Irish Treaty. The Dáil voted to ratify the Treaty by 64–57 votes on 7 January 1922. On each day of the debates, an overflowing gallery listened to impassioned speeches. All six female TDs rejected the Treaty, though it was supported by the majority of the leadership of the IRA.

Little trace of the building's former role as a university remains today. A stained-glass memorial window to Kevin Barry, unveiled by Éamon de Valera in the 1930s and depicting Robert Emmet, Patrick Pearse and other celebrated nationalist figures, has been moved in recent years to the new UCD campus at Belfield, four kilometres to the south of the city centre.

6 | BAGGOT STREET

Continue along Earlsfort Terrace away from the green. The next five locations of significance are all associated with one of the most notorious events of the War of Independence: Bloody Sunday, 21 November 1920. As the conflict wore on, the British were forced into deploying military intelligence agents in Dublin. The IRA, at the behest of Michael Collins, who saw the value of intelligence as a means of maximising the IRA's ability to combat a much larger and better resourced enemy, resolved to identify and assassinate a large number of them in one fell swoop. This came after the IRA in the capital had been relatively inactive or ineffective for a number of months. On the morning of Sunday 21 November the Dublin IRA, whose numbers had been augmented by other IRA members from outside the city, shot dead fourteen suspected and actual British military intelligence officers in the their lodgings around the city, and wounded a number of others. We will pass the venues for five of those killings along this stretch of this walk, beginning with 28 Earlsfort Terrace, where Captain John J. Fitzgerald was shot dead in his bed on 21 November. Born in Tipperary, he came from a prominent GAA family. A veteran of both the British

Army and Royal Flying Corps, he served in the Allied invasion of Russia in 1919 and joined the RIC after being demobilised, apparently with an eye to joining a colonial police force. He was in Dublin recuperating from injuries sustained in an IRA attack on the RIC barracks in Clare to which he had been posted.

Turn left onto Hatch Street. Follow it until it meets Leeson Street, then cross onto Upper Pembroke Street and continue along the street. On your left you will come to number 28, which was used as a lodging house by military personnel. Two intelligence officers, Charles Dowling and Leonard Price, were shot dead here, while a third, Hugh Montgomery, died of his wounds some weeks later; the latter was one of the most senior British military casualties of the War of Independence.

> *When I arrived at Upper Pembroke St. on the Sunday morning, I met [Paddy] Flanagan and a few other Volunteers. I explained to Flanagan that we had no keys for the hall doors in order to gain admission, so we went over our arrangements. Fortunately, at the zero hour of 9 a.m., the hall door was open and the porter was shaking mats on the steps. There were separate staircases in this double house and a party proceeded up either staircase to the rooms already indicated. I accompanied Flanagan and two other Volunteers to a room at the top of the house occupied by two officers, one of these being Lieut. Dowling. We knocked at the door and pushed it open. The two officers were awake in bed. They were told to stand up and were then shot.*

Charlie Dalton of the IRA's 'Squad' recalls the killings of British officers (Dowling and Price) on Pembroke Street on Bloody Sunday, 21 November 1920. Military Archives BMH WS 434.

Continue on to Baggot Street and turn right, walking away from the city centre towards the Grand Canal. This area, developed in the late eighteenth and early nineteenth centuries, was part of the old Pembroke estate, and forms part of what is the best-known Georgian district of the city. Two more houses on Baggot Street were the sites of killings on Bloody Sunday. Geoffrey

Bagalley, a court-martial officer who had lost a leg in the First World War, was killed at 119 Lower Baggot Street, while another court-martial officer, William Newberry, was killed in front of his wife at number 92.

The majority of those killed by the IRA on the morning of Bloody Sunday died in and around the south inner city. Not all of them were, in fact, agents, and many got away. But it was an enormous propaganda coup for the IRA and had knock-on effects: intelligence officers tended to reside in barracks after Bloody Sunday, which blunted their effectiveness.

Continue south-east along Baggot Street, towards the Grand Canal. At 67 Lower Baggot Street, a plaque commemorates Thomas Davis, a central influence over the revolutionary generation, most especially Patrick Pearse.

Davis, born in Mallow in County Cork in 1814, was an unlikely Irish separatist, being the son of a Protestant Welsh surgeon who worked with the Royal Artillery. Following the death of his father, his family relocated to Lower Baggot Street. He attended Trinity College Dublin, and involved himself in Daniel O'Connell's Repeal movement. In time, he was one of the founders of the Young Ireland movement, which split from the reformist O'Connell. Its newspaper, *The Nation*, championed 'a nationality which may embrace Protestant, Catholic, and Dissenter, Milesian and Cromwellian, the Irishman of a hundred generations, and the stranger who is within our gates.' Lady Jane Wilde, mother of Oscar, was among its contributors.

Turning left at Baggot Street Bridge, head towards Mount Street Bridge, a key battle site of Easter Week.

7 MOUNT STREET

The bridge over the Grand Canal at the junction of Mount Street and Northumberland Road, in Dublin's south inner city, was the scene of the heaviest and bloodiest engagement of the Easter Rising. The junction forms part of a natural route leading from south Dublin into the city centre along Merrion Square, terminating at Trinity College. As British reinforcements began to arrive at the southern ferry port of Kingstown (now Dún Laoghaire), this was the route they would take, and it presented an ambush opportunity.

On Wednesday 25 April, as members of the 176th and 178th Infantry Brigades (Sherwood Foresters) travelled along Northumberland Road, en route to Trinity College, they were ambushed by members of the 3rd Battalion of the Irish Volunteers, located in a number of buildings in the district, including 25 Northumberland Road, Carisbrooke House and Clanwilliam House (the latter has since been destroyed). These were narrow Victorian streets; Northumberland Road and the bridge across the canal formed a bottleneck that restricted the movement of troops. The British lost perhaps as many as 235 dead and wounded at this junction, as fighting continued in the area until 9pm that night. Various hospitals in the area were used to treat the wounded. A number of the Volunteers were also killed in the fighting: a memorial to Michael Malone forms part of the exterior stonework on 25 Northumberland Road. He was briefly buried in the garden of the house and was later interred in Glasnevin Cemetery's republican plot. A memorial to the engagement is located at the south side of the bridge over the canal.

Troops seem to have proceeded with caution for their rest of their route to Trinity, firing into some of the houses on Mount Street as they did so.

> *Half the battalion didn't believe it: many a one had no razor in his kit when the next chance to shave came. For the trains that we really did entrain into sped off not south-westward for the Plain of France, but away and away up the "North Western", and it wasn't until they dis-gorged us on Liverpool Docks that rumours could be swapped about Sinn Fein gentry – broken bottles and shillelaghs.*
>
> *It was a baptism of fire alright, with flintlocks, shot-guns, and ele-phant rifles, as well as more orthodox weapons. And 100 casualties in two days' street fighting was a horrible loss to one battalion: the more so since my one friend from the ranks, commissioned same day, was shot through the head leading a rush on a fortified corner house, first day on active service, and it was my job to write and tell his mother, who thought him still safe in England.*

> *Captain A.A. Dickson of the Sherwood Foresters recalls the engagement at Mount Street, in John Lewis (ed.),* True World War One Stories *(London, 1999).*

WALK 3, STOP 7 ■
*The view across Mount Street looking south
along Northumberland Road, 1952.
The Easter Rising memorial is visible to the
right. (Courtesy of Bureau of Military History,
Military Archives, Cathal Brugha Barracks)*

8 | BOLAND'S MILLS

Continue north along Clanwilliam Place and turn left onto Grand Canal Street; this was the location of Boland's Mills, near Grand Canal Dock and overlooking the Grand Canal itself; the current Treasury Building is on the site of the original mill. This complex of buildings was seized by members of the 3rd Battalion of the Irish Volunteers led by Éamon de Valera; perhaps as few as 100–130 poorly armed Volunteers were involved.

Boland's Mill was to serve as the headquarters of the Volunteers in a large region of Dublin's south inner city that was quite diverse in socio-economic terms and incorporated commercial and industrial regions in Dublin's docklands. The residential districts within the area seized by the Volunteers ranged from slum tenements near the docks to the middle-class residential districts in and around Merrion Square, and between the canal and Ballsbridge. The location of the area was significant, as it contained important transport links that connected Dublin to the southern ferry port of Kingstown, i.e. the rail terminus at Westland Row and the roads leading into the city that crossed the Grand Canal at Mount Street. There were plans to seize a number of buildings within the district, but these were curtailed. The Volunteers established outposts outside Beggars Bush Barracks, near Mount Street Bridge, and near Westland Row, where rail tracks were torn up in order to disrupt rail transport.

Continue along Grand Canal Street, heading away from the canal, and turn left up Holles Street. This is the location of the National Maternity Hospital; like many of the older hospitals in this part of the city, it was pressed into service to cater for casualties from the fighting in 1916, though it continued to carry out its regular duties as well.

9 | ORIEL HOUSE

Turn right at the top of Holles Street, onto Merrion Square itself, and walk west along the square until you reach the next junction. Turn right and walk past the Davenport Hotel. Directly in front of you will be a red-brick Victorian building: Oriel House, at the intersection of Fenian Street and Westland Row, is a building of great importance to the story of the Civil War in Dublin. Home to the semi-autonomous Criminal Investigation Department (CID), founded by Michael Collins in early 1922 and staffed by former IRA members loyal to him, including veterans of the 'Squad', it became synonymous with the sometimes brutal interrogation of republican prisoners and with the extrajudicial execution of prisoners. Under the stewardship of Joe McGrath, the CID were faced with the task of monitoring and dealing with political opponents of the new state; for many republicans, the CID was an institution to be feared, with good reason.

Oriel House was a somewhat doubtful institution, and a good many suggestions were made that its methods were too like the worst we hear of the American police. However, the American police operate under peace conditions, whereas Oriel House at the time was carrying on under war conditions, and if investigators were sometimes somewhat tough with prisoners, I should say that the circumstances were such that tough methods were not only excusable but inevitable.

Ernest Blythe defends the tactics associated with Oriel House. A former member of the Irish Volunteers and a Sinn Féin TD, during the Civil War Blythe was a minister in the first Free State government. Military Archives BMH WS 939.

In the autumn of 1922, four mines were planted in the basement of the CID building, though only one exploded. Simultaneously, republicans opened fire on the building, but retreated when the CID returned fire. As time went on, the excesses of CID and the Military Intelligence units in Wellington Barracks gradually saw them being sidelined from late 1922 onwards, though extrajudicial killings remained a feature of the conflict even after it officially ended in April 1923.

Turn left at Oriel House, and then right onto Westland Row. Continue north to the train station.

10 PEARSE STATION, WESTLAND ROW

Renamed in honour of Patrick and William Pearse for the Golden Jubilee of the Easter Rising in 1966, Westland Row station first opened in 1834, and its beautiful bridge dates from 1891. Westland Row witnessed huge gatherings for returning Easter Rising prisoners, at Christmas 1916 and into the following year.

When Countess Markievicz returned home in June 1917, she was met by the Fintan Lalor Pipe Band, and a huge procession made their way from here to Liberty Hall. These scenes were indicative of changing feeling on the ground in the capital, and stood in stark contrast with much of the immediate, hostile civilian response to the Rising.

At last, we reached Westland
Row. We were back in Dublin
city. One of the first men whom I
saw on the platform was Michael
Collins ... Volunteers lined the
platform, to try and keep back
the crowds, but they might as well
have been trying to keep back the
waves of the sea. We could not
get out of our carriages. Eventually, the Volunteers succeeded in
getting a passageway down the
stairs, and, in the street when we
emerged, the scene beggars
description. The people of
Dublin appeared to have crowded
themselves into one street, and
we were actually carried and
placed out on the wagonettes.
As we were recognised by old
Volunteers, whom I had last
seen when being marched out
of Richmond Barracks and de-
ported to England. They called
out our names in greeting, and
the crowds joined in. Volumes of
cheering, old friends of the
football and hurling teams all
tried to get near to us and
shake our hands.

WALK 3, STOP 9 ■
*Oriel House, home of the Criminal
Investigation Department during
the Civil War.*

*Gerard Doyle of the Irish Volunteers recalls
his release from captivity in June 1917.
Military Archives BMH WS 1511.*

PEARSE FAMILY BUSINESS, 27 PEARSE STREET

At the junction of Westland Row and Pearse Street, turn left and make your way back in the direction of College Green, where this walk began.

On your right will be 27 Pearse Street. The building houses the Ireland Institute, though as its restored signage shows, it was once Pearse & Sons, the family business of James Pearse. Father of Patrick and William, James was born in London in 1839 and raised in Birmingham in a Unitarian household. He studied in a Birmingham art school and in the 1860s moved to Dublin where he became a leading figure in sculpture. He specialised in ecclesiastical and architectural sculptures. Though immensely proud of his father, Patrick Pearse was conscious of his background, maintaining that 'two very widely remote traditions – English and Puritan and mechanic on the one hand, Gaelic and Catholic and peasant on the other ... worked in me and fused together by a certain fire proper to myself ... [and] made me the strange thing I am.'

Pearse & Sons was wound up in 1910, with the capital being utilised to help establish Patrick Pearse's innovative school St Enda's, near Rathfarnham, where he and his brother subsequently worked.

*The family home
and business
premises of the
Pearse family,
today the Ireland
Institute.*

12 PEARSE STREET GARDA STATION

One could see some bizarre sights from the windows during that week: corner-boys wearing silk hats, ladies from the slums sporting fur coats, a cycling corps of barefooted young urchins riding brand new bicycles stolen from some of the shops, and members of the underworld carrying umbrellas. One citizen was carrying a large flitch of bacon on his back, with another walking behind cutting off a piece of bacon with a large knife. Although the detectives, in common with the whole D.M.P. force, were by Commissioner's orders confined to barracks, members of the housebreaking squad were revolted at the sight of so much stolen property being flaunted before their eyes.

Eamon Broy, of the DMP (and future IRA intelligence agent) describes 1916 looters from the windows of Great Brunswick Street (now Pearse Street) station. Military Archives BMH WS 1280.

C ontinue east along Pearse Street until you reach the Garda station at the junction with College Street. This was once Great Brunswick Street police station, occupied by the Dublin Metropolitan Police. Note the carvings of heads of officers and constables of the DMP in the stonework of the building. Intelligence files on

WALK 3, STOP 12
Detail of carving of a Dublin Metropolitan Police officer in the stonework of Pearse Street Garda Station.

■ WALK 3, STOP 13

Plaque marking the offices of Irish Freedom, *the newspaper of the Irish Republican Brotherhood.*

leading republicans were kept in this building, and despite what Neil Jordan's film *Michael Collins* suggests, it was here and not in Dublin Castle that Collins succeeded in reading his own intelligence file, when the sympathetic DMP officer Eamon Broy gave him access to the building in April 1919.

This police station was a base for the much-feared G Division of the DMP, an intelligence-gathering force tasked with monitoring the 'movement of extremists' in the city. Founded in the nineteenth century in response to the Fenians, 'G Men' were an inevitable sight at any 'advanced nationalist' gatherings in the city.

On 3 September 1919, Detective Daniel Hoey was shot in the immediate vicinity of this building on Collins' orders. Hoey had been central to identifying leading republicans after the Rising, including Seán Mac Diarmada who almost evaded the authorities and seemed destined for internment in Britain. Detective Sergeant John Barton, who had also been involved in identifying prisoners after the Rising and who had since become a hate figure for republicans, due to his assiduous pursuit of them, was also shot dead near the station, again on the order of Collins, on 29 November 1919.

The counter-intelligence operations of the IRA, as orchestrated by Collins, owed much to the presence of agents such as Broy and David Neligan. Both men were among those leaking information to the republican movement. Apparently, one reason the killing of police officers became strictly vetted by the IRA as the conflict intensified was owing to the sheer number of them who proved sympathetic to the republican cause. There was nothing to be gained from unwittingly killing a potential, or actual, ally.

13 FENIAN OFFICES, D'OLIER STREET

Crossing from Pearse Street Garda Station onto D'Olier Street, a plaque at number 12 marks the location of the offices of *Irish Freedom*, the newspaper of the Irish Republican Brotherhood. Founded in 1910, the newspaper was the public expression of a secret revolutionary underground movement.

Founded in Dublin and New York City on St Patrick's Day 1858, the oath-bound movement popularly known as the Fenians had considerable influence in Irish American life in particular. James Stephens, a founding Fenian and the self-described 'Provisional Dictator' of the body, built contacts with radical movements across the continent and beyond, even proclaiming that 'were England a republic battling for human freedom on the one hand, and Ireland leagued with despots on the other, I should, unhesitatingly, take up arms against my native land.'

The abortive Fenian uprising in 1867 had an important influence on many of the 1916 leaders, who stood in the same tradition. The 1867 proclamation, sent to *The Times* in London, was, ironically, a more radical document than that read out at the GPO in 1916, with a very definite separation of Church and state and a rallying cry that 'Republicans of the entire world, our cause is your cause. Our enemy is your enemy. Let your hearts be with us. As for you, workmen of England, it is not only your hearts we wish, but your arms. Remember the starvation and degradation brought to your firesides by the oppression of labour.'

A bombing campaign in London followed in the 1880s, primarily brought about by the determination of Jeremiah O'Donovan Rossa, an exiled Fenian leader based in the United States. Thomas J. Clarke was imprisoned for his participation in the so-called dynamite campaign. By the early twentieth century, the IRB movement was in decline. By 1910, it was estimated to have as few as a thousand members in its ranks. Dan Breen dismissively recalled a generation who had become 'great fellows for talking and drinking and doing very little after that'. However, a younger generation of political radicals such as Bulmer Hobson, Dennis McCullough and Seán Mac Diarmada were crucial to the reorganisation of the secret society. Here at D'Olier Street, the IRB newspaper *Irish Freedom* was edited by Mac Diarmada, literally a stone's throw from the watchful eye of the DMP. The paper was highly seditious, maintaining that 'Our country is run by a set of insolent officials, to whom we are nothing but a lot of people to be exploited and kept in subjection. The executive power rests on armed force that preys on the people with batons if they have the gall to say they do not like it.' Unsurprisingly, the newspaper was suppressed in 1914.

To begin the fourth walk, make your way down D'Olier Street and turn right at the River Liffey, crossing over the Rosie Hackett Bridge.

WALK 4 THE NORTH INNER CITY

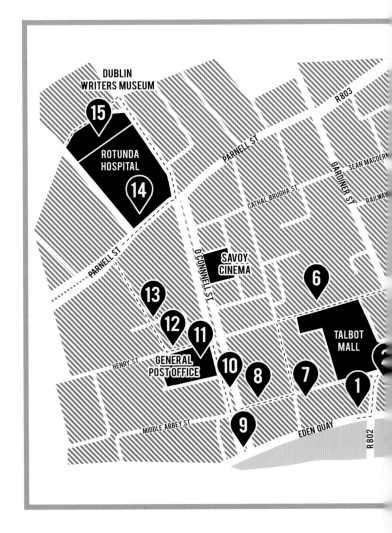

DUBLIN
WRITERS MUSEUM

15

ROTUNDA
HOSPITAL

14

PARNELL ST

R 803

GARDINER ST

SEAN MACDERM

CATHAL BRUGHA ST

RAILWAY

PARNELL ST

O'CONNELL ST

SAVOY
CINEMA

6

13

12   11

TALBOT
MALL

HENRY ST

GENERAL
POST OFFICE

10   8

7

1

MIDDLE ABBEY ST

9

EDEN QUAY

R 802

Introduction

This walk crosses back over to the northern side of the River Liffey. While it is the shortest of the walks in this book, it is by far the most iconic, as it traverses some of the areas and locations that played host to some of the most important events, not just of the Irish revolution in Dublin, but of the revolution as a whole.

1. LIBERTY HALL

2. JAMES CONNOLLY STATUE

3. CUSTOM HOUSE

4. 44 GARDINER STREET AND MOLLY O'REILLY PLAQUE

5. 'MONTO'

6. TALBOT STREET

7. THE ABBEY THEATRE

8. WYNN'S HOTEL

9. O'CONNELL STREET

10. JAMES LARKIN STATUE

11. THE GPO

12. 21 HENRY STREET, IRISH FARM PRODUCE COMPANY

13. HENRY STREET, MOORE STREET AND O'RAHILLY PARADE

14. THE ROTUNDA

15. PARNELL SQUARE

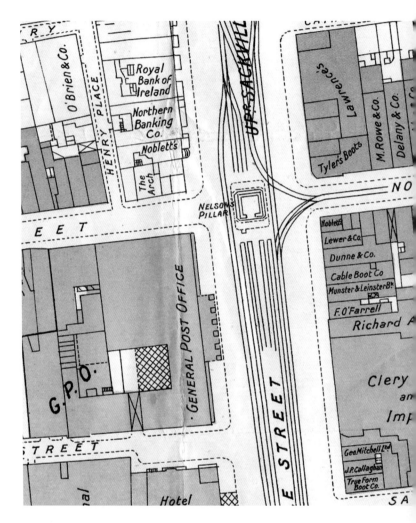

■ **WALK 4**
*Dublin Fire Brigade Chief Officer Thomas Purcell's map detailing the destruction
of Sackville Street. The buildings in red were all destroyed by fires.
(With thanks to Dublin Fire Brigade Museum)*

ARL STREET

E PLACE

WALK 4 ◼

*The Daniel O'Connell monument
on O'Connell Street includes
numerous bullet holes, proof of
the fighting of Easter Week.*

1   LIBERTY HALL

We begin this walk at Beresford Place, just outside Liberty Hall. Spanning sixteen floors, Liberty Hall is an impressive feature of the Dublin skyline. Gilroy McMahon's 1960s building is very different architecturally from its previous incarnation in the early twentieth century. Liberty Hall was originally the Northumberland Hotel, located just north of the River Liffey on Beresford Place, facing the Custom House. It became the headquarters of James Larkin's ITGWU in 1912 and subsequently the headquarters of the Irish Citizen Army after its foundation in 1913. The policies and activities of the ITGWU were often dubbed 'Larkinism' by their opponents. Under Larkin it espoused an Irish variation of syndicalist trade unionism, which first made its presence felt in Belfast in 1907 when Larkin arrived there as an organiser with the National Union of Dock Labourers. The dock strike of 1907 has achieved something of a legendary status in Irish labour history, with Larkin bridging the sectarian divisions in the city to such an extent that unionist and nationalist bands paraded together through the Falls and Shankill Roads.

In the aftermath of the Belfast dispute, Larkin established the ITGWU. It believed in organising workers across a wide range of industries, and creating a single trade union which would represent the interests of the

CHANCELLOR DUBLIN

■ **WALK 4, STOP 1**
A contemporary postcard showing the damage done to Liberty Hall in the aftermath of the Easter Rising.
(Courtesy of Dublin City Library and Archives)

HALL . HEAD-QUARTERS OF CITIZEN ARMY, DUBLIN.

working class as a whole. In this regard, it was much like the Industrial Workers' of the World (the IWW or the 'Wobblies', as they were popularly known) in the United States, which championed the slogan 'One Big Union'. Both Larkin and James Connolly were involved with the IWW during stints in the United States.

■ **WALK 4, STOP 1**
Reformed Irish Citizen Army
at Liberty Hall, 1917.
(Courtesy Military Archives,
Cathal Brugha Barracks)

The ITGWU also placed an emphasis on building a working-class cultural life, in a manner that impressed more sympathetic observers. *The Manchester Guardian* was so moved by Larkin's project on visiting Liberty Hall that in November they proclaimed 'no labour headquarters in Europe has contributed so valuably to the brightening of the lives of the hard-driven workers around it ... it is a hive of social life'.

Later described by *The Irish Times* as 'the centre of social anarchy in Ireland, the brain of every riot and disturbance', Liberty Hall had been a focal point for radical politics for a number of years prior to the Easter Rising of 1916. When Herbert Asquith and John Redmond addressed a recruiting meeting in the Mansion House in September 1914, a large labour contingent assembled at Liberty Hall to march to an anti-conscription protest at St Stephen's Green addressed by both Larkin and Connolly; at one point during the First World War it was famously adorned with a banner reading 'We serve neither King nor Kaiser but Ireland'.

In the weeks and months leading up to April 1916, Liberty Hall was used to manufacture and store weapons, and hosted lectures on military planning. James Connolly lectured on urban insurrectionism here, studying cases like the Paris Commune of 1871 and the Moscow insurrection of 1905. The 1916 Proclamation was printed in Liberty Hall on the presses of Connolly's newspaper *The Workers' Republic*, and on 24 April 1916 it became the assembly point for those insurgents who actually took part in the outbreak of the Rising. The building was damaged by artillery and was raided by the military during the Rising, though it was not destroyed.

The building is adorned with a number of memorials. On the Eden Quay side, notice the memorial to the Irish

LIBERTY HALL
THIS FOUNDATION STONE
WAS LAID ON THE 12TH OF
MAY 1962 BY JOHN CONROY
GENERAL PRESIDENT OF
THE IRISH TRANSPORT AND
GENERAL WORKERS' UNION
Ní saoirse go saoirse lucht oibre

■ WALK 4, STOP 1
Foundation stone of Liberty Hall, today home to SIPTU.

Citizen Army in the lobby of the building, which can be read from the street. Stepping into the lobby, we can read the names of members of the Citizen Army taken from the organisation's own membership roll. On the Beresford Place side of the building, a commemorative plaque honours the Irish Women's Workers' Union, founded in 1911 by Delia Larkin, sister of Jim and a formidable union organiser in her own right. Abbey Theatre actor and Citizen Army member Helena Molony was secretary of the body from 1915, while Jacob's biscuit factory worker Rosie Hackett was a member from the early days of the body. A nearby bridge spanning the River Liffey is named in her honour.

2 | JAMES CONNOLLY STATUE

Cross the road to the other side of Beresford Place and turn left, stopping at the statue of James Connolly by Eamon O'Doherty. The monument was unveiled in 1996 and funded in no small part by the Irish and American labour movements. Born to Irish parents in the slums of Edinburgh's Cowgate in 1868, Connolly enlisted in the British Army at the age of fourteen, serving in Ireland with the 2nd Battalion of the Royal Scots Regiment. He was subsequently active in radical politics in Scotland, working alongside his brother John in the Scottish Socialist Federation and later joining the Independent Labour Party, formed by Keir Hardie. He was invited to Dublin in 1896 by Adolphus Shields of the short-lived Dublin Socialist Club. Connolly became the (sometimes) paid organiser of the fledgling body. He founded the Irish Socialist Republican Party later that same year, fusing Irish separatism and socialism.

Connolly was a prolific and influential writer and between 1903 and 1910 was also active in American labour politics, in particular with the Industrial Workers' of the World and the Socialist Party of America. In 1910 he published *Labour in Irish History*, an ambitious Marxist survey history of Irish society. On his return from the United States, Connolly was centrally important to Liberty Hall and the ITGWU, and while his relationship with Larkin was an uneasy one, they formed a formidable political alliance. Following Larkin's departure for the United States in 1914, in the aftermath of the defeat of the labour movement in the 1913 Lockout, Connolly assumed control over the ITGWU and the Irish Citizen Army. His decision to bring the Citizen Army into the 1916 Rising divided radical opinion, with Seán O'Casey later maintaining that Irish labour had sacrificed itself at the altar of Irish nationalism. Seamus McGowan of the Citizen Army would later recall Connolly telling the body to 'hold onto their rifles' in the event of victory, as a workers' republic remained their aspiration.

The monument incorporates the words of Connolly himself, taken from an article written weeks before the Rising and published in *The Workers' Republic*, where he insisted that 'the cause of labour is the cause of Ireland, the cause of

ISE OF LABOUR IS THE CAUSE OF IRELAND   THE CAUSE OF IRELAND IS THE CAUSE OF

WALK 4, STOP 2
'The cause of Ireland is the cause of Labour'
– commemorative statue of James Connolly,
Beresford Place.

Ireland is the cause of labour.' The backdrop for the monument is the Starry Plough, flag of the Citizen Army. Connolly maintained that 'a free Ireland would control its own destiny, from the plough to the stars'. It remains an important symbol to the Irish left and the union movement, and the original flag is today on display in the National Museum of Ireland, Collins Barracks.

Connolly was executed in Kilmainham Gaol on 12 May 1916 for his role in the Easter Rising. On the first anniversary of his execution, a banner appeared on Liberty Hall, reading 'JAMES CONNOLLY: MURDERED MAY 12 1916'.

3 | CUSTOM HOUSE

Behind Connolly's monument stands James Gandon's masterpiece, the Custom House. Constructed between 1781 and 1791, the building shifted the economic axis of the eighteenth-century city. It was designed to be seen from all sides; the massive Doric south front is 375 feet wide. A statue of Commerce rests upon the dome, but a notable feature are the carved keystone heads, representing Ireland's rivers, of which Anna Livia – the Liffey – is the only female head. It housed a wide range of goverment offices in the nineteenth century, including the emigration office. In the early twentieth century it housed the local government department before independence. The best view of the building is provided from Custom House Quay, looking at its southern façade, so walk back towards the River Liffey and turn left to begin a circuit of the building. Notice the royal coat of arms on either side of the building, today a relatively unusual sight in the Irish capital.

Its role as the headquarters for the Local Government Board for Ireland during the revolutionary period made it a target, and the building was burnt down on 25 May 1921 in a daring operation orchestrated by the 2nd Battalion of the Dublin Brigade of the IRA, acting under the command of Tom Ennis and Oscar Traynor. This spectacular attack was conceived of as a propaganda exercise; the burning the building was a success and also resulted in the destruction of paperwork vital to the establishment of local government functions. On the other hand, the operation resulted in the deaths of five IRA men, as well as the capture of more than 80 members of the Dublin IRA.

> *The crowds which had gathered outside the barbed wire barriers erected by the military watched the progress of the fire until curfew hour. About this time several shots were fired, and in a few minutes the streets were deserted. The firing of the shots, it was understood, was for the purpose of forcing some doors which could not be opened by other means. About this time shooting was heard in other parts of the city, and also the sounds of what appeared to be two bomb explosions, but no explanation could be obtained last night.*

During the night troops were quartered in Liberty Hall, which is within the enclosed area, and outside this building field kitchens were drawn up. In addition to the soldiers at the barriers, sentries were posted in the streets leading to the Custom House. The curfew patrols displayed much activity, and seventeen persons were arrested ... The firemen continued to work throughout the night, but despite their efforts the fire continued to burn fiercely ... The dome still stands, and it is interesting to note that at least up until eleven o'clock last night the clock had not stopped, but had registered the correct time.

The Irish Times, *26 May 1921.*

The destruction of the building owed much to collusion between the IRA and the men of the Dublin Fire Brigade, some of whom had even provided advice to the IRA on how to burn the building. The brigade proved less than enthusiastic when it came to tackling the blaze. Firefighter Joseph Connolly, a captain in the Irish Citizen Army, recalled spreading paraffin to parts of the building that were not burning when the brigade arrived. It was thanks to fire brigade assistance that Michael O'Kelly of the Citizen Army was able to enter the Custom House, survey the extent of the damage there, and crucially organise the removal of pistols and revolvers from the building.

You can see a legacy of the destruction if you look up: the stonework on the dome is darker than the stone on the rest of the building. This is a legacy of its reconstruction in the 1920s, when Irish limestone was used to repair the dome, rather than the original Portland stone (much of the interior had to be completely rebuilt as well).

Walking to the rear of the building, we find the work of the Breton sculptor Yann Renard Goulet RHA. This 1956 memorial shows a stylised figure of Éire (Ireland) and a dying soldier, confirming the ironic point often made that the Custom House is a rare example of a building that comes with a memorial to people who successfully destroyed it.

WALK 4, STOP 3 ■
Monument to the Dublin Brigade IRA at the rear of the Custom House.
(Courtesy Las Fallon)

WALK 4, STOP 3 ■
Captain Joseph Connolly,
Irish Citizen Army and
Dublin Fire Brigade.
(Courtesy Las Fallon)

■ WALK 4, STOP 3
*A dramatic account of the burning of
the Custom House from a contemporary
French magazine.
(Courtesy Las Fallon)*

4 44 GARDINER STREET AND MOLLY O'REILLY PLAQUE

Cross Beresford Place onto Gardiner Street, walking under the railway bridge. At number 44, a memorial plaque honours Molly O'Reilly, a small reminder of the role played by Irish women in the independence movement. As a teenager, O'Reilly raised a symbolic green flag over Liberty Hall shortly before the 1916 Rising. Later, during the War of Independence, while working in the prestigious United Services Club at St Stephen's Green, she provided information to Michael Collins, in his capacity as the IRA's Director of Intelligence. The plaque was erected during the 1916 centenary by the North Inner City Folklore Project, and notes Molly's later role in the revolutionary movement.

5 | 'MONTO'

Continue to walk north along Gardiner Street, turning right at the junction with Talbot Street. This is very close to the large Victorian red-light district known as 'Monto'. Continue walking and turn left onto James Joyce Street, where a plaque upon The Lab art space remembers local publican Phil Shanahan, a Tipperary man and a veteran of the 1916 Rising whose pub was an important rendezvous and place of refuge for the IRA in the War of Independence. The Lab itself is located on the junction with Foley Street, formerly Montgomery Street; this is what the nickname 'Monto' was derived from. The area was sustained by its proximity to the docks and the military installation at nearby Aldborough House, not to mention a sizeable coterie of visitors from elsewhere. It was notorious enough to warrant a mention in the *Encyclopaedia Britannica* of 1903, which proclaimed that 'Dublin furnishes an exception to the usual practice in the UK. In that city the police permit open houses confined to one street; but carried on more publicly than even in the south of Europe or in Algeria.' James Joyce immortalised the area by including it in *Ulysses*, albeit as 'Nighttown'.

> *The lady prostitutes used to pinch the guns and ammunition from the Auxiliaries or Tans at night, and then leave them for us at Phil Shanahan's public house. I might add that there was no such thing as payment for these transactions, and any information they had they gave us.*

> Dan Breen, Military Archives BMH WS 1739.

The demise of Monto came in 1925, when the district was raided by the Garda Síochána following lobbying by the Catholic lay group the Legion of Mary, led by Frank Duff (who, in fairness, was motivated to some degree by concerns for the women being exploited in the area by pimps and madams, as well as by Catholic morality).

6 | TALBOT STREET

Retrace your steps back onto Talbot Street and turn right, walking in the direction of O'Connell Street, Dublin's main thoroughfare. The 121m tall Monument of Light (or 'Spire') in the distance will guide you. At 94 Talbot Street, a plaque erected by the National Graves Association honours Tipperary republican Sean Treacy. This premises was known as the 'Republican Outfitters' during the revolutionary period, dressing the men and women of the IRA, Cumann na mBan and other radical organisations. Treacy had been one of those who carried out the Soloheadbeg Ambush in County Tipperary on 21 January 1919, when two RIC constables were killed as Treacy and Dan Breen sought to hijack a cart of explosives belonging to a local quarry. This took place on the same day that Dáil Éireann met for the first time in Dublin, and the Soloheadbeg attack is generally taken to mark the beginning of the War of Independence, though the event occurred without the sanction of Dáil Éireann. Treacy was followed into the Republican Outfitters by intelligence officers on 14 October 1920. Both he and Lieutenant Gilbert Price were shot and killed during a gunfight outside the premises.

This plaque was unveiled in 1937 by Andy Cooney, who had served as Chief of Staff of the IRA in 1925. When Tipperary qualify for the All-Ireland hurling final, there is a tradition of fans gathering here on the morning of the game for a short commemorative ceremony.

7 | THE ABBEY THEATRE

Continuing up Talbot Street, turn left onto Molesworth Street, which is home to the Abbey Theatre. Walking towards the River Liffey, you will find the Abbey Theatre at the intersection of Lower Abbey Street and Molesworth Street.

Michael Scott's 1966 Abbey Theatre bears no resemblance architecturally to the theatre founded by William Butler Yeats, Lady Gregory and others in 1904. Today it is the official national theatre, and the Abbey was at the heart of the cultural revival that swept nationalist Ireland in the years before the revolution. This 'revival' manifested itself in literary, artistic, cultural (such as attempts to revive the use of Irish as a vernacular), sporting (such as the GAA) and political forms, and was driven by a widespread sense among younger nationalists that Ireland was losing its distinctive cultural characteristics, and was becoming little more than a derivative provincial offshoot of Britain. The multifaceted cultural revival was intended to reverse this trend, and the Abbey Theatre was perhaps the most famous manifestation of this revivalism, though it was not without its critics; its 1907 production of J.M. Synge's *The Playboy of the Western World* was disrupted by nationalist protestors who viewed it as a stage-Irish mockery of the Irish peasantry and a slur on Irishwomen.

Cultural nationalism often went hand in hand with political nationalism: a number of Abbey actors and staff directly participated in the Easter Rising, including the first female lead of the theatre, Máire Nic Shiubhlaigh, and the popular actor Seán Connolly, killed on the roof of City Hall on the first day of the insurrection.

Prior to fighting in the Rising, Abbey actor Arthur Shields (son of Adolphus Shields) visited the theatre to collect his rifle, which was hidden beneath its floorboards. In a curious twist of fate, Shields later acted in John Ford's *How Green Was My Valley,* the 1951 Academy Award-winning picture. Also starring in the film was John Loder, who (as Lieutenant John Lowe) had fought to suppress the 1916 Rising and stood beside his father, General William Lowe, in the iconic image of Pearse's surrender.

Inside the lobby of the theatre today, a memorial unveiled by Taoiseach Seán Lemass (himself a 1916 veteran) on the fiftieth anniversary honours some of those associated with the theatre who participated in the Rising, while upstairs paintings by John Butler Yeats honour the founders of the theatre, including his own son.

Following on from the Irish revolutionary period, the Abbey Theatre remained an important space for those wishing to engage with the Irish revolution intellectually, though again, this did not always meet with approval. The theatre hosted *The Plough and the Stars* in 1926, a Seán O'Casey play which criticised the revolutionary nationalists who planned and executed the Rising and emphasised the poverty of the Dublin of the time. The play was interrupted and heckled by protesting republicans, including the well-known feminist campaigner Hanna Sheehy-Skeffington. On the other hand W.B. Yeats, who was never shy of placing himself front and centre, declined O'Casey's equally acerbic anti-war play *The Silver Tassie*, seemingly on the ground that its subject matter – Irishmen fighting and suffering in the First World War as soldiers in the British Army – was an inconvenient topic that complicated a simpler story of the revolution as a straight fight between Ireland and Britain.

8 WYNN'S HOTEL

Heading up Lower Abbey Street towards O'Connell Street, we pass Wynn's Hotel. Opened in 1845, the hotel was the setting for two important meetings during the revolutionary period. Inside the hotel, a plaque commemorates a meeting held here on 11 November 1913, where the decision to establish the Irish Volunteers was taken. Among those to attend that meeting were Patrick Pearse, Michael O'Rahilly ('The O'Rahilly'), Eoin Mac Neill and Seán Mac Diarmada. MacNeill, a co-founder of the Gaelic League (established in 1893 to promote the revival of the Irish language) and professor of Early Irish History at University College Dublin, had called for the formation of an Irish nationalist volunteer body in response to the emergence of the UVF.

Later, Wynn's Hotel was the location for the founding meeting of Cumann na mBan, presided over by UCD Irish lecturer Agnes O'Farrelly, and another plaque in Wynn's commemorates their foundation. The organisation stated its objectives were, amongst other things, to 'advance the cause of Irish liberty', to 'organise Irish women in the furtherance of that objective', and to 'assist in arming and equipping a body of Irish men for the defence of Ireland'. The latter ensures that Cumann na mBan is often described as simply a women's auxiliary force to the Irish Volunteers, but it evolved into a formidable political force in its own right. As Mary Colum, a founding member of the body, maintained: 'we are not the auxiliaries or the handmaidens or the camp followers of the Volunteers – we are their allies.'

Cumann na mBan members were active participants in the Easter Rising (though not as combatants) and in the revolutionary period that followed, and the body overwhelmingly opposed the Anglo-Irish Treaty of 1921. A minority of early members, including the veteran activist Jennie Wyse Power, would establish a pro-Treaty women's organisation entitled Cumann na Saoirse. The willingness of some Irishwomen to carve out a space for themselves in the independence movement was also intertwined with the ongoing struggle for suffrage, in the form of the right to vote in parliamentary elections.

During the Easter Rising, Wynn's Hotel was gutted by the fires that swept Lower Abbey Street. During the First World War, the Methodist church across from Wynn's housed a 'soldiers' rendezvous', providing non-alcoholic refreshments and facilities for troops.

9 O'CONNELL STREET

From Wynn's, we enter O'Connell Street (formerly Sackville Street), home to the GPO and thus central to the story of the Easter Rising and, indeed, much of the Irish revolution as a whole. It began life in the eighteenth century as an enclosed residential mall, which explains its unusual width. Over time, it evolved into a thoroughfare and was, by the beginning of the twentieth century, a commercial and retail district. The street is now named in honour of constitutional nationalist leader Daniel O'Connell, whose bullet-riddled monument stands at the bottom of the street overlooking the River Liffey. The work of sculptor John Henry Foley, the 1880 monument depicts Hibernia herself pointing towards O'Connell, standing on broken chains to symbolise the achievement of Catholic Emancipation in 1829. Bullet holes can be clearly seen across the statues, and the sword held by one of the winged figurines is missing: small reminders of what happened here in 1916. The variegated architecture of the southern end of the street is a much larger, but indirect, reminder of the Rising. In the course of Easter Week 1916 the British Army fired artillery into this district, causing devastating fires; most of the southern end of O'Connell Street had to be reconstructed in the aftermath.

10 JAMES LARKIN STATUE

Walking up the central traffic island towards the Monument of Light (the 'Spire'), we pass the monuments to William Smith O'Brien (a member of the Young Ireland movement) and Sir John Gray (the man responsible for the introduction of a clean water supply to the Irish capital). James Larkin takes pride of place near the centre of the street, with Oisín Kelly's 1978 statue depicting the labour leader as he was in life. The west side of the monument includes a verse from the Monaghan-born poet Patrick Kavanagh:

> *And Tyranny trampled them in Dublin's gutter*
> *Until Jim Larkin came along and cried*
> *The call of Freedom and the call of Pride*
> *And Slavery crept to its hands and knees*
> *And Nineteen Thirteen cheered from out the utter*
> *Degradation of their miseries.*

WALK 4, STOP 9 ■
Sackville (now O'Connell) Street prior to the Easter Rising.
(Courtesy Dublin City Library and Archives)

The location of the statue is tied into the events of 31 August 1913, during the 1913 Lockout. Larkin sought to address a banned meeting from the balcony of the Imperial Hotel (on the site of the Clery's building); this was owned by William Martin Murphy, the transport magnate who had taken the lead in banning membership of Larkin's ITGWU from his tram companies. Larkin, in disguise, entered the hotel and made his speech, but the crowd was attacked by members of the DMP from Princes Street, directly beside the GPO.

> *Suddenly the cry was heard, 'a baton charge', and immediately there was utter confusion. The whole street, or the people who were, unfortunately, traversing it, was set in motion. People ran hither and thither, the police on their heels chasing them. No time to ask questions, how or why this happened? I found myself, like other folk, running away from a group of policemen who were behind us wielding their batons. I made to get into one of the side streets and away from the excitement and, of course, the batons. But at every point that I tried to breach there was a sturdy posse of police in possession to drive us back into O'Connell Street and worst luck for some, into the line of fire of the police batons.*

Seán Prendergast, Military Archives BMH WS 755.

11 | THE GPO

The General Post Office (GPO) on O'Connell Street is the most famous location associated with the Easter Rising. Designed by Francis Johnston and opened in 1818, the GPO was seized by members of the Irish Volunteers and Irish Citizen Army led by Patrick Pearse and others early on the afternoon of 24 April 1916. Johnston was also responsible for the Nelson Pillar, which stood where the Spire is today (the GPO's now bullet-scarred columns may have been intended to echo the larger monument). At an imposing 121 metres, the Spire, erected in 2003, is much taller than Horatio Nelson's

WALK 4, STOP 9 ▪
Postcards of the ruins of Sackville St after the Rising
(Courtesy of Dublin City Library and Archives)

memorial, which predated London's Nelson Column and which included a viewing platform over the metropolis. The pillar met its end on 8 March 1966, when a group of republicans, formerly members of the IRA, placed an explosive device in its staircase, in what one might describe as an unofficial fiftieth anniversary tribute to the Easter Rising. Nelson's head survives in the reading room of Dublin City Library and Archive on Pearse Street, where he keeps his one good eye firmly fixed on the researchers.

For a great view of the GPO, the traffic island is unrivalled. Notice the flags flying over the building today. In 1916, a green flag bearing the words 'Irish Republic' flew from the south-east corner of the building, and the tricolour from the north-east corner. The original 'Irish Republic' flag is today on display in the National Museum of Ireland, Collins Barracks. The proclamation was read by Pearse in the location today occupied by the clock in the centre of the building, then the main entrance. (The document was printed in Liberty Hall on the eve of the insurrection, using type borrowed from another printer in Capel Street; the printer, Christopher Brady, had been employed at Liberty Hall since 1915, where he printed *The Workers' Republic* newspaper and union materials for the ITGWU.) Like so many building associated with the Rising, the facade of the GPO still bears the marks of small-arms fire.

Below the clock, in the central window of the building is Oliver Sheppard's monument 'The Death of Cúchullain', linking the 1916 Rising to the warrior hero of Irish mythology, who died facing overwhelming odds; it is an apt metaphor, considering how the Rising came to be viewed after the fact. The monument was unveiled by Éamon de Valera in 1935, who described it as 'a beautiful piece of sculpture, the creation of Irish genius, symbolising the dauntless courage and abiding constancy of our people'.

The GPO was the headquarters of the Easter Rising. A well-worn joke claims that the number of those who claimed to have fought in it could easily fill a stadium such as Croke Park, but thanks to the painstaking work of Jimmy Wren, we now know that perhaps over 520 men and women were in the GPO during the Rising. Among them were the majority of the 'Provisional Government' leaders who signed the Proclamation. James Connolly was wounded while inspecting barricades in the vicinity, crawling back to the GPO in agony through the nearby Williams Lane, today at the rear of Penney's department store, which stands on the site of the Metropole Hotel, another rebel outpost during the Rising.

The rationale for seizing the GPO remains unclear, but it was a key communications hub in Dublin. It was also a very visible symbol of official authority north of the River Liffey, and its location on the wide expanse of Sackville Street ensured that its seizure, and thus the outbreak of the rebellion itself, would be widely observed. It had both a practical and propaganda value, and so the GPO became the headquarters garrison for the insurgents. In the early days of the Rising many observers noted an almost surreal atmosphere, complete with looters and sightseers, in the vicinity of the GPO. O'Connell Street was a commercial street that adjoined some of the worst slums in the city; given that the DMP were withdrawn from the streets at a relatively early stage, there was ample opportunity for looting to take place, though it should be said the poor were not the only looters.

/ *Noblett's, at the corner of Earl Street, and Lemon's, in Lower Sackville Street, were titbits for the younger section of the roughs, who made merry with boxes of chocolates, sweets, etc, all the afternoon. The toyshops were also centres of great activity, and then having exhausted Lower Sackville St the crowds swept around into Earl St and Henry St, where they found an abundance and variety that suited every taste. Boys and girls were swaggering about, dressed in the most fantastic apparel, and all had their arms full of mechanical and other toys, hockey and golf sticks, and all kinds of articles used in popular pastimes.* /

The Irish Times *reports on the looting in the early days of the Easter Rising, from* The Sinn Fein Rebellion Handbook *(Dublin, 1917).*

WALK 4, STOP 9 ■
The remains of the Nelson Pillar, 1966. (Courtesy Pól Ó Duibhir)

As the week wore on, the fighting intensified, and O'Connell Street was bombarded with artillery, which caused devastating fires to break out in the commercial district around the GPO. Oscar Traynor, a member of the Irish Volunteers (and later Minister for Defence) recalled looking out the windows of the Metropole on the fourth day of the Rising, and having 'the extraordinary experience of seeing the huge plate-glass windows of Clery's stores run molten into the channel from the terrific heat'.

/ *The white letters of the words "Irish Republic" on its surface gradually scorch a deep brown hue. Now and then it is buried in an upheaval of thousands of fragments of burning paper ... during four days and nights it has flown above the building proudly and defiantly; it now begins to hang its head as if in shame. At nine o'clock the GPO is reduced to ruins. Its four granite walls look like the bones of a skeleton skull. Its core is nothing but smouldering debris. The fluttering of the flag grows feebler. In the dimness of the night I see it give an occasional flicker, as if revived by the gust of air. At length at 9.51pm, the staff supporting it begins to waver and in a second falls out towards the street.*

—————— /

An anonymous account of the destruction of Sackville Street, from Mick O'Farrell, 1916: What The People Saw *(Cork, 2013).*

■ **WALK 4, STOP 9**
The Dublin Fire Brigade work amidst the destruction, Easter 1916.
(Courtesy Las Fallon)

Owing to its burning roof and the fear of its imminent collapse, the GPO was abandoned towards the end of the Rising (it did not reopen until 1929 and most of what exists behind the facade is a reconstruction). Williams and Woods factory, on King's Inns Street, was the first poured-concrete building in the city, and was earmarked as the destination for the GPO garrison. Today, 'ghost signs' on the building recall its former life, though it is now an art space known as The Chocolate Factory. To get to the factory, however, the rebel forces would have to make their way through a labyrinth of laneways and side streets. They did so by leaving the GPO's side door and making their way across Henry Street.

■ **WALK 4, STOP 10**
*Detail from the James Larkin
monument.*

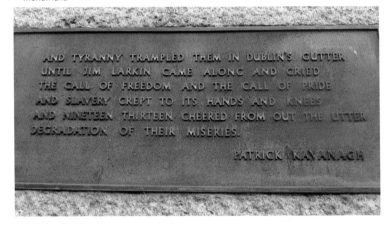

WALK 4, STOP 10 ■
The Irish Worker *cartoon remembering
the violence of Bloody Sunday, 1913.
(Courtesy Military Archives, Cathal Brugha Barracks)*

POBLACHT NA H EIREANN.

THE PROVISIONAL GOVERNMENT

OF THE

IRISH REPUBLIC

TO THE PEOPLE OF IRELAND.

IRISHMEN AND IRISHWOMEN : In the name of God and of the dead generations from which she receives her old tradition of nationhood, Ireland, through us, summons her children to her flag and strikes for her freedom.

Having organised and trained her manhood through her secret revolutionary organisation, the Irish Republican Brotherhood, and through her open military organisations, the Irish Volunteers and the Irish Citizen Army, having patiently perfected her discipline, having resolutely waited for the right moment to reveal itself, she now seizes that moment, and, supported by her exiled children in America and by gallant allies in Europe, but relying in the first on her own strength, she strikes in full confidence of victory.

We declare the right of the people of Ireland to the ownership of Ireland, and to the unfettered control of Irish destinies, to be sovereign and indefeasible. The long usurpation of that right by a foreign people and government has not extinguished the right, nor can it ever be extinguished except by the destruction of the Irish people. In every generation the Irish people have asserted their right to national freedom and sovereignty ; six times during the past three hundred years they have asserted it in arms. Standing on that fundamental right and again asserting it in arms in the face of the world, we hereby proclaim the Irish Republic as a Sovereign Independent State, and we pledge our lives and the lives of our comrades-in-arms to the cause of its freedom, of its welfare, and of its exaltation among the nations.

The Irish Republic is entitled to, and hereby claims, the allegiance of every Irishman and Irishwoman. The Republic guarantees religious and civil liberty, equal rights and equal opportunities to all its citizens, and declares its resolve to pursue the happiness and prosperity of the whole nation and of all its parts, cherishing all the children of the nation equally, and oblivious of the differences carefully fostered by an alien government, which have divided a minority from the majority in the past.

Until our arms have brought the opportune moment for the establishment of a permanent National Government, representative of the whole people of Ireland and elected by the suffrages of all her men and women, the Provisional Government, hereby constituted, will administer the civil and military affairs of the Republic in trust for the people.

We place the cause of the Irish Republic under the protection of the Most High God, Whose blessing we invoke upon our arms, and we pray that no one who serves that cause will dishonour it by cowardice, inhumanity, or rapine. In this supreme hour the Irish nation must, by its valour and discipline and by the readiness of its children to sacrifice themselves for the common good, prove itself worthy of the august destiny to which it is called.

Signed on Behalf of the Provisional Government,

THOMAS J. CLARKE,
SEAN Mac DIARMADA, THOMAS MacDONAGH,
P. H. PEARSE, EAMONN CEANNT,
JAMES CONNOLLY. JOSEPH PLUNKETT.

WALK 4, STOP 11 ◼

The Proclamation of the Irish Republic, issued on 24 April 1916.

■ WALK 4, STOP 11
Above: The clock of the GPO.
(Courtesy Las Fallon)

Right: Looking in
the window of the GPO,
Easter 2016.
(Courtesy Luke Fallon)

12   21 HENRY STREET, THE IRISH FARM PRODUCE COMPANY

Turning onto Henry Street, a plaque on 21 Henry Street, just past the GPO, commemorates the location where the 1916 Proclamation was signed.

This site was home to the Irish Farm Produce Company, a shop and restaurant (specialising in vegetarian cuisine) run by veteran nationalist

campaigner Jennie Wyse Power. It was popular with Dublin's small Indian community (and perhaps even smaller vegetarian community) but owing to its proprietor it also became a rendezvous point for advanced nationalists.

Jennie Wyse Power, born in Baltinglass in 1858, moved through the ranks of many important political movements in her lifetime, and had earned the respect of the men and women who frequented her business. Active in the Ladies' Land League of the 1880s, which sought to advance the rights of Ireland's tenant farmers, she was later a founding member of Sinn Féin and close to Constance Markievicz. While serious about her politics, Wyse Power was also regarded as one of the friendliest faces in Irish nationalism. Sinn Féin Executive member Seamus ua Caomhanaigh remembered that 'she always left out the Wyse part of her name. She said there was nothing 'wise' about her. She was a remarkably able woman, very brainy, full of fun and a great teller of humorous stories.' The restaurant remained a hub for republicans throughout the revolutionary period.

Dublin's small Indian community, primarily formed from medical students in the city, would be drawn towards Wyse Power's restaurant too, at a time when there was little in the line of vegetarian offerings in the city. Dublin's first vegetarian restaurant, The Sunshine (advertised as 'vegetarian dining rooms'), had opened its doors in the 1860s on Grafton Street, though such endeavours tended to be short-lived. Indian students in the capital during the revolutionary period included V.V. Giri, later President of India, who studied under the poet and revolutionary separatist Thomas MacDonagh. As Conor Mulvagh has suggested, 'in searching for routes of entry for Indian students into Irish radical politics, it is perhaps the dinner table as much as the lecture theatre that provided them with introductions'. The cause of the Indian people received sympathetic coverage in Irish nationalist newspapers, including Arthur Griffith's *Sinn Féin* and *The Irish Volunteer*.

While Cumann na mBan flatly rejected the Anglo-Irish Treaty of 1921, Jennie Wyse Power came to support it, which created friction between her and many former comrades. In 1923, her business premises was entered by young men who at first appeared to be ordinary customers, but 'as the tea was about to be served the raiders suddenly took petrol bottles from their pockets and announced their intention of setting the house on fire'. Her other business premises, located on Camden Street, had already been attacked by republicans, with 'bombs being hurled through the plate glass window'.

Notice the plaque includes an Easter lily, a symbol created in 1926 by the anti-Treaty Cumann na mBan, sales of which were intended to raise much-needed funds as well as being as a form of remembrance for those who had given their lives in the Rising.

13 HENRY STREET, MOORE STREET AND O'RAHILLY PARADE

Cross to the northern side of Henry Street, where it is still possible to walk the evacuation route taken by the republican garrison in 1916 after they were forced to abandon the building.

WALK 4, STOP 12 ◼

The site of the Irish Farm Produce Company, where the 1916 proclamation was signed.

> *We evacuated in small groups, and dashed across Henry Street into Henry Place, which was right across from the Henry Street exit gate of the Post Office. At Henry Place, we were confronted by machine guns, fire apparently from the Rotunda. We took cover and, in small numbers, turned the corner to reach the Moore Street houses; and, as each party dashed across the opening of Moore Lane, machine gun fire came down the lane. We all got across in safety.*

Fintan Murphy, Military Archives BMH WS 370.

Henry Place (the first right off Henry Street), which turns left onto Moore Street, and Moore Street itself were the immediate destinations for the insurgent forces. If you glance up at the red-brick facades on Henry Street, near the junction with Moore Street, you will notice the date 1917 carved into one of the buildings; a small sign of reconstruction, as this street was devastated in the fighting as well. Turn right into Moore Street, and pause at Moore Lane, which is the first right turn. This is the continuation of Henry Place, and was one of the routes used by the GPO garrison to escape. A British machine-gun position on Great Britain Street (today Parnell Street) at the Rotunda Hospital had a clear line of sight on the rebels as they crossed Moore Lane, though a cart was used to block the lane and the insurgents broke into the terrace of red-brick houses on the northern side of Moore Street, killing a young civilian, Bridget McKane, when one of the Volunteers shot through a door to gain entry to 10 Moore Street, at the end of the terrace. From here they contemplated their next move, but were desperately short of supplies. The British took the Rising extremely seriously, and had thrown a cordon around the city centre; this ran along Parnell Street, at the end of Moore Street. Despite trying to tunnel through the terrace of buildings on Moore Street, it became obvious to the insurgents that they were trapped and a decision to surrender was ultimately taken at 16 Moore Street, marked by a humble plaque from the 50th anniversary in 1966 of the Rising. To reach it, continue walking along Moore Street, heading away from Henry Street and towards Parnell Street.

WALK 4, STOP 13 ■

Top: Commemorative plaque to The O'Rahilly,
marking the location of his death.
(Courtesy Las Fallon)

Bottom: A lane near the surrender location of the GPO
garrison is named in The O'Rahilly's honour.
(Courtesy Las Fallon)

Numbers 14 to 17 Moore Street, where the garrison as a whole took refuge, will be on your right.

Continue walking towards Parnell Street, and turn right into O'Rahilly Parade, formerly Sackville Lane, which is adorned with a large and distinctive memorial. Among those killed in the evacuation of the GPO was Michael Joseph O'Rahilly, known as The O'Rahilly. A founding member of the Irish Volunteers and its Director of Arms, he was centrally important to the landing of rifles at Howth in 1914. Though O'Rahilly had attempted to stop the insurrection – delivering news of Eoin MacNeill's countermanding order to the south of Ireland – he himself participated in the fight when it came. O'Rahilly died, having taken a number of bullets, in a doorway in Sackville Lane; the plaque (which replaced an earlier, smaller one erected by the National Graves Association) reproduces his last letter to his family, written as he lay dying in the lane. Rendered in a facsimile of his own handwriting, it is difficult to read, but this is its wording:

'Written after I was shot – Darling Nancy. I was shot leading a rush up Moore Street. Took refuge in a doorway. While I was there I heard the men pointing out where I was + I made a bolt for the lane I am in now. I got more one bullet I think. Tons + tons of love dearie to you + to the boys + to Nell + Anna. It was a good fight anyhow. Please deliver this to Nannie O'Rahilly, 40 Herbert Park Dublin.
Good bye darling.'

Hoping to negotiate terms, the leaders of the Rising were told by the British that only an unconditional surrender would be accepted. Leaving the building, Pearse made his way to a British barricade in the company of Elizabeth O'Farrell of Cumann na mBan, surrendering to Brigadier General William Lowe on 29 April. The image of Pearse, wearing his slouched hat (not unlike the Boer guerrillas of the early twentieth century) and long coat before Lowe is one of the iconic images of the Rising. It is often suggested that O'Farrell was airbrushed from the photo, though she herself stated in 1956 that she had stepped back to avoid being photographed. Ironically, for all its fame (or notoriety as a supposed metaphor for the treatment of women in independent Ireland), it is unclear where exactly the surrender took place on what is now Parnell Street.

◢ *At 2.30 pm Commandant-General Pearse surrendered to General Lowe accompanied by myself and Lieutenant Lowe at the junction of Moore Street and Great Britain Street. He handed over his arms and military equipment. His sword and automatic repeating pistol in holster with pouch of ammunition, and his canteen, which contained two large onions, were handed to me by Commandant-General Pearse.*

◢

Captain Henry de Courcy-Wheeler's account of Pearse's surrender, from Alex Findlater (ed.), 1916 Surrenders: Captain De Courcy-Wheeler's Eyewitness Account *(Dublin, 2016).*

14 THE ROTUNDA

Following Pearse's surrender, the survivors of the GPO marched back to O'Connell Street, thence to the north end of the street to be detained in the grounds of the Rotunda Hospital. Continue to the end of Moore Street and turn left onto Parnell Street, crossing the road to the hospital, which was founded in the 1740s. The car park was originally a garden, which is where the prisoners were held overnight before being marched out to Kilmainham and Richmond Barracks. Some, notably Tom Clarke, were subjected to ill treatment whilst being detained there.

A small plaque in the grounds honours the Volunteers held here after the Rising. Across the street from the Rotunda gardens, Conway's pub is deserving of brief mention – it had the misfortune of falling victim to the looters of Easter Week, who remain a key feature of the folklore of the Rising (though perhaps it was a predictable target). Sadly, at the time or writing, the pub remains closed.

Continue along Parnell Street and stop at the Ambassador – formerly the Rotunda Rink – which on 25 November 1913 hosted the first public meeting of the Irish Volunteers, and which throughout late 1916 also housed the postal services that had previously been based in the destroyed GPO. The plaza in front of it offers a useful vantage point along Parnell Street and the northern end of O'Connell Street. Across the junction, at the corner of Parnell Street and O'Connell Street, was Thomas J. Clarke's newsagents, today occupied by a Londis shop. A veteran Fenian, Clarke was the most senior man to sign the 1916 Proclamation.

Born in England in 1858, Clarke was the son of James Clarke, a sergeant in the British Army. Raised in Dungannon, County Tyrone, he became an active Fenian at the age of twenty in 1878, later settling in the United States. He spent fifteen years in British prisons for his actions during the Fenian dynamite campaign of the 1880s, becoming one of the last Fenian prisoners in British institutions. Following his eventual release he returned to the United States, where he married Kathleen Daly, before returning to Ireland in 1907. In Dublin, Clarke opened two tobacco shops and newsagents. One was located on Amiens Street, the other on Parnell Street. It is not surprising, given his history, that these shops were closely monitored by the authorities. The shop sold Irish nationalist and radical newspapers, and advertisements for papers such as *Irish Freedom* and *The Workers' Republic* were often to be found outside the shop. Constance Markievicz recalled that 'the little shop at the corner of Parnell Street

■ **WALK 4, STOP 14**
Detail in the water feature of the Garden of Remembrance.

was so handy, that one could always find a moment to run in and hear what he had to say on any trouble or complication that might arise', though it was constantly monitored by the DMP.

The monument of Parnell at the junction of Parnell Street and O'Connell Street (pointing the way, one might say, to Conway's), which is the work of American artist Augustus Saint Gaudens, was unveiled by nationalist leader John Redmond in 1911. The monument includes Parnell's claim that 'no man has a right to fix the boundary to the march of a nation'. In many ways, Redmond came even closer than Parnell to achieving the dream of a constitutional solution to the Irish question in the form of Home Rule. On the day after Redmond unveiled the monument, *The Freeman's Journal* proclaimed that 'If we are on the threshold of Home Rule, no man is more accountable for that fact than Parnell'. On 31 March 1912 O'Connell Street was the venue for a mass rally in support of Home Rule that was addressed by John Redmond, Tom Kettle, Eoin MacNeill, and Patrick Pearse, amongst others, speaking from four platforms arranged on the street.

O'Connell Street has a surface area exceeding seven and a half acres, and it was thought that a space so large would have held the vast assembly. It was a vain hope ... The side of Rutland Square, behind, and Parnell Street and Britain Street, at the other side of the noble monument, were crowded for considerable distances with eager, pressing throngs. When the momentous assembly had come together, the sight, looking up O'Connell St from the south side of the bridge, was an amazing one. It was a vast sea of heads, filling up all between the house lines, and relieved only by the five monuments and the four platforms, with their green decorations.

The Freeman's Journal *(1 April 1912) reports on the vast Home Rule rally of 31 March 1912.*

The Parnell monument was also the spot where British soldiers (from, ironically, the Royal Irish Regiment) posed with the captured 'Irish Republic' flag following the Rising, and Parnell himself has an Easter Week bullet in his shoe.

From the same vantage point, one can see the rather stern block of buildings on the eastern side of O'Connell Street. These are also reconstructions, though the originals were not destroyed in the Easter Rising; rather, they were attacked during the outbreak of the Civil War, in June 1922. Attempting to divert attention from the Four Courts, anti-Treaty IRA men under the command of Oscar Traynor seized a number of buildings on O'Connell Street, including the Gresham and Hammam hotels. They were joined by members of the Irish Citizen Army, acting under the command of John Hanratty. 'The Block', as it was nicknamed, stretched from roughly the modern Cathal Brugha Street to Cathedral Street. Following the Free State capture of the Four Courts, this area was attacked by machine-gun fire, armoured cars and artillery; the top of Henry Street was one of the vantage points used by Free State forces. Traynor's republican forces had tunnelled through the buildings throughout the 'block'; most of the anti-Treaty IRA had abandoned it by 3 July, with a small force under Cathal Brugha remaining and retreating to the Granville Hotel, at the centre of the 'block'. By this time the buildings were on fire and Brugha ordered his men to surrender, though refused to do so himself; he was fatally wounded as he emerged, firing, from the ruins. He was buried in Glasnevin Cemetery and is commemorated by the newer street that bears his name. The buildings that constituted the 'block' were rebuilt in a somewhat austere style in the 1920s, with the Savoy Cinema, opened in 1929, being a notable new addition.

15 PARNELL SQUARE

We head eastwards from the Rotunda around the Ambassador Theatre and turn north onto Parnell Square (originally Rutland Square). Some significant markers at Parnell Square include a small stone memorial to mark the foundation meeting of the Irish Volunteers, located just west of the Garden of Remembrance. In Irish, it marks the 25 November 1913 meeting which saw more than 3,000 men enlist in the new body. In the run up to the meeting, Patrick Pearse had proclaimed that 'Ireland unarmed will attain just as much freedom as it is convenient for England to give her; Ireland armed will attain ultimately just as much freedom as she wants'. Within months of this meeting, the Volunteer movement would be split by war on the continent, as John Redmond urged them to enlist in the British Army.

> *In addition to the 4,000 people in the hall a crowd of 3,000 were unable to gain admission. The path from Cavendish Row down to the entrance of the hall was a steep slope and were much afraid that the pressure of people would smash in the doors which had been closed. Traffic in Cavendish Row was blocked by the crowds, and [Seán] MacDermott and some others went out and addressed them.*
>
> *Amongst those who spoke were [Eoin] MacNeill, who acted as chairman, Laurence J. Kettle and P.H. Pearse. I decided not to speak as I was looked upon by many people as being very extreme. It is interesting that at the beginning of the Volunteers, P.H. Pearse warned Eoin MacNeill of the danger of allowing extreme nationalists like me to gain control of the Volunteer movement.*

> *Bulmer Hobson recalls the founding of the Irish Volunteers, 25 November 1913: F.X. Martin (ed.),* The Irish Volunteers, 1913–15: Recollections and Documents *(Dublin, 1966).*

The vast majority of the movement sided with Redmond, calling themselves the Irish National Volunteers; the rump opposing him kept the original name (the Irish National Volunteers took some 140,000 men from the movement, leaving the Irish Volunteers with a body of under 10,000). From the beginning, the Volunteer movement was a curious mix of radical separatists and constitutional nationalists, and while the movement was committed to Home Rule (on paper at least) there was a strong republican faction within it from its earliest days.

Across the street is 10 Parnell Square, formerly the Fowler Memorial Hall, used by the Orange Order and a focal point for loyalist opposition to Home Rule in the pre-war period. It was also the base of the Dublin Loyal Volunteers, an armed anti-home rule militia modelled on the UVF which claimed to have 2,000 members in Dublin city and county in the pre-war period; they subsequently became a 'Volunteer Training Corps' during the First World War. The hall itself was seized by the anti-Treaty IRA in early 1922 and was used to house Catholic refugees from Belfast. In 1935 it housed the parcel section of the post office; a minor renovation revealed a large cache of over 90 rifles along with gospel tracts.

Continue to walk to the north of Parnell Square, to the Garden of Remembrance. This is the centrepiece of the square, opened on the Golden Jubilee of the Rising in 1966. Designed by Dáithí Hanly, the garden is dedicated to the memory 'of all those who gave their lives in the cause of Irish Freedom.' Within its sunken cruciform water feature are mosaic depictions of ancient Gaelic weaponry, symbolising a custom of casting weapons into rivers after battles. A sculpture of the mythical Children of Lir by Oisín Kelly was added to the garden in 1971.

In 2007, a new entrance was added to the northern side of the garden, ideal for those wishing to visit the neighbouring Dublin Writers Museum or Hugh Lane Gallery, both of which hold works dealing with the Irish revolutionary period. The gallery has another link to the revolution. Hugh Lane, after whom it was named, was an art collector who had offered to bequeath his collection to the city of Dublin on the condition that a gallery be built to house it. The campaign against what was seen as a potential waste of public money prompted W.B. Yeats to write one of his most famous poems, 'September 1913'. Lane died in May 1915 when the liner *Lusitania* was torpedoed by a German U-boat off County Cork; an arrangement was eventually made to house some of his collection in the old Georgian townhouse of the Earl of Charlemont, which is now the Hugh Lane Gallery.

Finally, on the western side of Parnell Square, numbers 29 and 30 remain curiously unmarked. They were once occupied by Vaughan's Hotel, which was an important meeting place for members of the IRA General Headquarters staff during the War of Independence, and was particularly associated with

Irish Rebellion – May 1916.
A group of Officers with the captured rebel flag.

WALK 4, STOP 15 ■

Above: Postcard showing the captured 'Irish Republic' flag at Parnell monument.

Left: Commemorative plaque to Thomas J. Clarke, on the site of his tobacco shop.

Michael Collins. The wedding reception of the leading Cork republican Tom Barry was held in Vaughan's, after the Truce of 1921. Many attendees, including Éamon de Valera, Michael Collins, Eoin O'Duffy and Barry himself, would find themselves participating in the eventual Civil War on opposing sides.

The fifth and final walk follows on directly from this one, beginning at Findlater's Church on the north-east of Parnell Square.

WALK 5 NORTHERN FRINGES

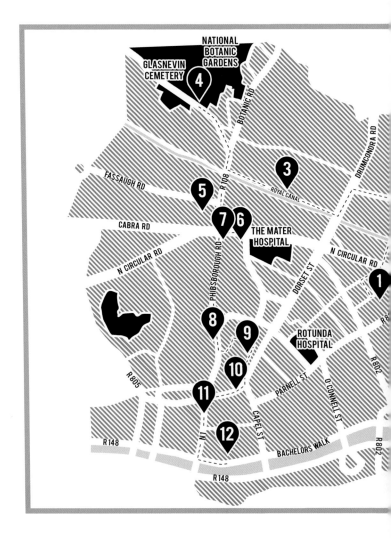

Introduction

The fifth and final walk begins in the north inner city and takes the form of an extended loop that runs out to the vast necropolis of Glasnevin Cemetery, back through Phibsborough before ending at the Four Courts, thereby bringing the extended route that the five walks collectively make up to an end near where the first walk began.

Begin this walk at the Gothic Revivalist Abbey Presbyterian Church (built in the 1860s and commonly dubbed Findlater's Church after the wealthy mercantile family who paid for it) at the north-east corner of Parnell Square.

We waited for about twenty minutes but nothing turned up. The streets were becoming more crowded with pedestrians enjoying the sunshine but we were very worried about their safety as enemy forces, when attacked, usually fired indiscriminately without regard to the lives of the passers-by. We could not, of course, warn the citizens of the danger, and had, perforce, to take a chance and hope that the ordinary people would remain unscathed. The lorry commenced moving in our direction very slowly and we prepared to attack it. The British troops were packed very tightly in the vehicle. When it reached Findlaters Church, the first ambush position, we opened fire and threw two hand grenades which landed right in the centre of the lorry. The occupants immediately started firing indiscriminately and a number of pedestrians were wounded. The lorry accelerated until it reached Dorset Street corner where it again came under attack from our men stationed there.

Michael O'Kelly of the Dublin Brigade of the IRA recalls a street ambush on British troops outside Findlater's Church, 1 June 1921. Military Archives BMH WS 1636.

Cross the road to Great Denmark Street. Walk along it, passing Barry's Hotel (a noted haunt of the anti-Treaty IRA in early 1922) and Belvedere College to get to Mountjoy Square.

At the outbreak of the civil war the first place attacked in the North side was the Fowler Hall which was occupied by the Republicans and which they had to leave. The morning of the attack William, my porter, went down to the rere of the building and climbed some steps to see what was happening. He poked his head in the door at the top of the steps. We were watching him and we saw him suddenly withdraw his head from a flying bullet. He had a narrow escape. The people inside the building thought he was one of the attacking party. He hastened back to us and within an hour our own hotel was occupied by the Republicans and the Citizen Army. Madame Markievicz was in charge of the Citizen Army and the leaders of the Republicans were there from time to time, including De Valera, Barton. I cannot remember the others. There were other women there too but I did not know them. This was on the Tuesday morning and the leaders were there till Wednesday night. They established their headquarters in the dining room. The first thing they did was to knock all the glass out of the doors and windows. They sandbagged the Windows and stuck guns out between the bags. They allotted different rooms to the various purposes. They cleared out all the visitors – about forty – giving them barely time to pack their bags. They cleared out the staff, but I refused to go and Miss Keogh and William the Porter stayed with me. The Headquarters Staff left on Wednesday night and took over the Hamman but they left a garrison in Barry's. The I.R.A. brought in oceans of food but I thought it queer that they did not want to give us any of it. We were not allowed to pass through the rooms they occupied. I cant remember how we put in our time during the occupation. I was half out of my mind thinking of all the money I owed the bank which financed the purchase of the hotel and I now saw the possibility of the whole place going up in smoke. This was the reason I refused to leave although they pointed out the risk I was running by staying.

Annie Farrington, the new owner of Barry's Hotel, records her experience of the outbreak of the Civil War. Military Archives BMH WS 749.

1 | MOUNTJOY SQUARE

Mountjoy Square was developed by Luke Gardiner, grandson of the Luke Gardiner who developed much of this part of the city in the Georgian era; he was killed serving with government forces at New Ross in Wexford in 1798. The square itself was built between 1793 and 1818. It was the last of Dublin's Georgian Squares, but is the only one to form a perfect square: the gardens measure 450 ft/14m on each side. By the 1840s it was a popular residence with the legal profession but, like much of the old Gardiner estate, went into steep decline thereafter and its profile had changed drastically by 1901. Many of the houses had been divided into multiple dwellings, and the square was occupied by a religiously diverse mix of students, domestic servants and skilled workers (many of whom were boarders); number 35, on the south side, was an orphanage in 1901. By 1920 it consisted of tenements, one of which was inhabited by the playwright Sean O'Casey; it may have inspired the setting for his play *The Shadow of a Gunman*. W.J. Stapleton of the 'Squad' later claimed that a raid on the house in early 1921 was the basis for the events of the play.

Number 3, on the northern side of the square, was the residence of Walter Cole, an alderman and leading member of Sinn Féin. Prior to the Easter Rising it was used for meetings by many of the signatories of the 1916 proclamation (including Clarke, Pearse, Connolly and Mac Diarmada). Cole himself was imprisoned in Britain for his role in the Rising, and the family of Seán Connolly apparently lived in the house for a period after the Rising. Its role as a venue continued during the War of Independence when it hosted meetings of the underground Dáil government and acted a safe house for leading republicans, including Collins and de Valera; Cole himself was arrested there in a raid in September 1920. Collins' Squad retained arms dumps in and around Mountjoy Square; in February 1921, the entire square was cordoned off and searched by the British Army, in an operation in which tanks were deployed. Such large-scale search were generally systematic, as British forces would work their way through selected districts in the city one at a time.

Mountjoy Square also has a literary association with two unexpected links to the revolution. In James Joyce's *Ulysses*, Father Conmee meets the wife of the real-life Home Rule MP David Sheehy (whose daughter Hanna married Francis

Skeffington, who was killed by a deranged officer during the 1916 Rising; another daughter, Mary, married the MP and academic Thomas Kettle, who was killed at the Battle of the Somme).

Continue around the square to Fitzgibbon Street and walk down it, crossing the North Circular Road to get to Jones's Road, thence to Croke Park.

2 | CROKE PARK

The modern Croke Park is the headquarters of the GAA and is unrecognisable from its revolutionary incarnation. The stadium is located on the site of the former 'City and Suburban Racecourse' on Jones's Road, whose owner, the city alderman Maurice Butterly, had sought to host a variety of sporting events on the site; it was mainly used for athletics events, and was also the original home of Bohemians FC. The GAA was the sporting manifestation of the late nineteenth-century cultural revival, founded at a time when field sports of various kinds (including cricket, rugby and soccer) were being codified and becoming increasingly popular; the fact that these were all of British origin prompted figures such as Michael Cusack to establish the association to provide a more distinctly Irish sporting alternative.

The ground that became Croke Park was first used by the GAA in 1892. At this time the GAA was consolidating its presence nationwide, but the lack of dedicated grounds was a major problem for the association, especially as it went through the doldrums in the 1890s before enjoying a revival in popularity from the turn of the century onwards. It hosted the Leinster football final between Meath and Dublin clubs in 1896; that year it also hosted the All-Ireland hurling and football finals, which had been delayed from the previous year. Having been placed on the market in 1907 after Butterly's death, it was sold to Frank Dineen in 1908 for £3,250 (most of which he borrowed). It was redeveloped with terraces, and the pitch was improved. The ground was bought by the GAA with the proceeds of an enormously successful tournament played in 1913 in memory of Thomas Croke, the Catholic archbishop of Cashel who was the association's first patron (Kerry beat Louth in the replayed final in front of a record crowd of 35,000 people). The treasurer, Luke O'Toole, moved swiftly to buy the ground from Dineen lest the funds be used to erect a statue of Croke in Thurles. The new ground was named after Croke to deflect clerical grumblings, and Thurles got its statue in 1920.

While many of the officials in the GAA at this time (such as O'Toole) leaned towards separatism, the GAA sought to steer a middle course between the competing wings of Irish nationalism and avoided the militarism of the pre-war volunteering movement. After 1916 the GAA became more overtly associated with separatism, being repressed by the British authorities: 'Gaelic Sunday' on 4 August 1918, when clubs nationwide played games in defiance of the British authorities, was a response.

Technically, nearly half of Croke Park consists of monuments to the revolutionary period, in the form of the Hogan Stand to the west of the ground and Hill 16, the terrace at the northern end. The latter gives rise to one of the enduring myths about the ground: for generations it was assumed to have been built from the rubble in O'Connell Street after the Easter Rising, which was scooped up and dumped against the railway embankment to create a new terrace; Hill 16 was the obvious name and gave the ground an enduring veneer of patriotism.

But don't let the facts stand in the way of a good story. The terrace existed in late 1915, in fact, long before the Easter Rising, and was originally dubbed Hill 60, after a hill in, of all places, Gallipoli. The ground was being redeveloped in 1915, and in August of that year, during the allied campaign in the Dardanelles, the Connaught Rangers suffered heavy casualties trying to take Hill 60 from its

■ **WALK 5, STOP 2**
Croke Park, pictured in 2015. (Courtesy Dennis Horgan

Turkish defenders. The name was attached to the embankment located (at that time) in the north-east corner of the ground. The 'Hill 16' myth only emerged in the 1930s; presumably, naming part of the stadium after an engagement in which the British Army had fought was deemed unseemly. And given other events in Croke Park during the revolution, this was perfectly understandable.

*The match was in progress for about ten minutes when
an aeroplane flew overhead and fired a Verey light signal.
Tipperary was playing Dublin on this occasion and the play
was concentrating about the Dublin goal. A penalty had been
awarded against the Dublin team and I was about to take the
free kick when a burst of machine-gun and rifle fire occurred.
The crowd of spectators immediately stampeded. The players
also fled from the field in among the sideline spectators,
except six of us who threw ourselves down on the ground
There we were. The six of us who remained – Hogan and I
and four of the Dublin team – were I think all Volunteers.
I suppose it was our Volunteer training that prompted us
to protect ourselves by lying down rather than by rushing
around. From where we lay, we could see sparks flying off
the railway embankment wall where the bullets struck the
wall, and we saw people rolling down the embankment who
presumably were hit. There was general pandemonium at
this stage between the firing, people rushing and a general
panic amongst the crowd. Two of the players who were lying
on the field at this stage got up and made a rush for the
paling surrounding the pitch on the Hill Sixty side, which was
nearest to them. One by one we followed their example, and
it was while Hogan was running from the field to the paling
that he got hit by a bullet. I think Josie Sinnott and myself
were the last to leave the field. Going across to Hogan, I tried
to lift him but the blood was spurting from a wound in his
back and I knew he was very badly injured. He made the
exclamation when I lifted him, "Jesus, Mary and Joseph! I am
done!", and died on the spot. My hands and my jersey were
covered with his blood.*

*Thomas Ryan, Tipperary footballer (and IRA member) recalls Bloody
Sunday in Croke Park and the death of his teammate Michael Hogan.
Military Archives BMH WS 783. (Coincidentally, a spectator killed along-
side Hogan was also called Thomas Ryan.).*

The imposing Hogan Stand is named after Michael Hogan, a Tipperary football player shot dead on the pitch by British forces during a match on 21 November 1920: Bloody Sunday. Following the killing of British officers around the city by the IRA that morning, Auxiliaries targeted the crowds attending a challenge football match being played by Dublin and Tipperary at Croke Park as part of the citywide crackdown. In what is generally assumed to have been little more than a reprisal, British forces began firing into the crowds of spectators from the Canal End, shooting dead a number of people and causing a stampede in which some were crushed and trampled to death; another was fatally wounded by spikes as he tried to clamber over a railing to escape. Nine were killed on the day, and five more died of wounds later; three of the dead were aged under fourteen. Hogan, the Tipperary captain, was a member of the IRA, though his death was due to the indiscriminate shooting. Another spectator, Thomas Ryan, was shot dead whilst kneeling to pray with the fatally wounded Hogan. More than anything else, the events of Bloody Sunday have fastened the association of Croke Park and the GAA with the revolution, though the GAA sought to avoid political dissension in the latter phases of the Civil War by banning collections and the sale of political literature from Croke Park.

Redeveloped from the 1990s and completed in 2005 with a capacity of 82,300, it is now one of the largest stadiums in Europe. The structure is truncated by the presence of the Royal Canal and railway lines at each end of the ground.

3 | THE ROYAL CANAL AND MOUNTJOY PRISON

Continue along Jones's Road, turning left at Clonliffe Road. Continue on and turn left onto Drumcondra Road, before turning right just before the Royal Canal. Cross Whitworth Road and join the grassy path alongside the Royal Canal, where the first thing you will meet is a statue of the writer Brendan Behan. Behan was the nephew of Peadar Kearney, the author of 'The Soldiers' Song' and part of the Jacob's garrison during the Easter Rising. Behan remembered that 'I was proud that the same blood ran in our veins.' Behan's father, Stephen, was active in the IRA during the War of Independence and the Civil War, eventually imprisoned in Kilmainham Gaol. Brendan Behan joined the IRA in his teens, and was imprisoned for his involvement in the disastrous 'S Plan' campaign, a bombing campaign of British cities. He achieved fame as a playwright and novelist, and died in March 1964, his heavy drinking eventually taking its toll. Joan Littlewood, the famed theatre director who had brought Behan's work to the stage in London, remembered him as 'the rumbustious wild boy' who could not be controlled. He is buried in the nearby Glasnevin Cemetery.

Eventually, on your left, on the other side of the canal, you will see the stern Victorian edifice of Mountjoy Prison. The Royal Canal was built between 1789 and 1809, and originally had a spur that veered to the west of the site of Mountjoy; one of the reasons for locating the prison here is that the two canal branches on either side of the site would add an extra layer of security. It was based on Pentonville Prison in London, which was designed as a pioneering 'model' prison that emphasised reform as well as punishment. The first prisoners were detained there in 1851. It housed republican prisoners from 1917 onwards, many of who went on hunger strike, demanding political status, in September 1917. Amongst these was Thomas Ashe, who died after being force-fed whilst on hunger strike in the prison on 25 September 1917.

On 14 May 1921, during the War of Independence, the IRA mounted an audacious but unsuccessful attempt to break the senior IRA commander Sean MacEoin out of the jail using a stolen British armoured car; they escaped under heavy fire and managed to avoid capture, only abandoning the armoured car when it ran out of petrol. The prison was the venue for numerous executions by the British authorities during the independence struggle, including that of Kevin Barry, and also by the Free State government during the Civil War, most notoriously those of Liam Mellows, Rory O'Connor, Richard Barrett and Joseph McKelvey. They were executed without trial on 8 December 1922 by order of W.T. Cosgrave's government as a reprisal for an IRA attack on members of the new Free State Dáil the previous day in which one, the veteran Cork IRA man Sean Hales, was killed.

 The executions reverberated in Mountjoy. I had been in the crowd outside the prison on the morning of a batch of executions in 1921 and the scene of utter helplessness was the most painful feature of that experience. But that sense of helplessness outside was a

■ **WALK 5, STOP 3**
Memorial statue to Brendan Behan. (Courtesy Paul Reynolds)

Protestors outside Mountjoy Prison, 23 July 1921. (Wikimedia Commons)

little thing compared with that one felt inside. Its immediate effect was to darken the whole jail with a brooding sense of vengeance that grouped men in cells.

Peadar O'Donnell remembers the 8 December 1922 executions in his prison memoir The Gates Flew Open *(Dublin, 1932).*

The prison was also used to house prisoners throughout the Civil War, becoming a venue for further republican hunger strikes in the process.

Continue along the canal until you reach Cross Guns Bridge, which marked the limit of the British cordon thrown around the city during and after the Easter Rising. Turn right at the bridge and take the left-hand fork in the road onto the Finglas Road. The wall of Glasnevin Cemetery will be on your left. Continue until you reach the main cemetery entrance.

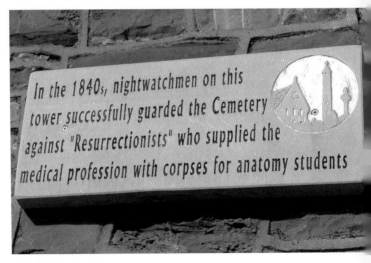

In the 1840s, nightwatchmen on this tower successfully guarded the Cemetery against "Resurrectionists" who supplied the medical profession with corpses for anatomy students

■ **WALK 5, STOP 4**
Commemorative plaque at Glasnevin Cemetery. (Courtesy Ciarán Murray)

WALK 5, STOP 4 ■
*Contemporary image of the 'republican plot' and the grave of Thomas Ashe
in Glasnevin Cemetery (Courtesy of Glasnevin Trust).*

4 GLASNEVIN CEMETERY

Glasnevin (originally Prospect) Cemetery is Dublin's largest cemetery, having opened in 1832. By the late nineteenth century the route that funerals took to the graveyard from the city centre followed the imposing wall along the Finglas Road (complete with watchtowers to protect against nineteenth-century grave robbers) and turned right into the area directly in front of the enormous tomb of Daniel O'Connell, who headed the committee that founded Glasnevin and its predecessor at Goldenbridge. Immediately to the left when entering the gate is the Sigerson Monument, designed by Dora Sigerson Shorter and erected amidst much acrimony in the 1920s as a memorial to the Easter Rising (it was originally located elsewhere in the cemetery). The

WALK 5, STOP 4
*The grave of trade unionist Jim
Larkin, Glasnevin Cemetery.
(Courtesy Ciarán Murray)*

more recent 1916 Remembrance Wall adjacent to the museum building lists all the victims of the Easter Rising: insurgents, British military personnel (a third of whom were, in fact, Irish), and civilians, who comprised nearly 55 per cent of the dead of the Easter Rising.

To the right of the O'Connell Tower is the single most famous section of the cemetery: the republican plot. Massive public funeral processions to Glasnevin Cemetery can be traced back to its origins as Prospect Cemetery in the 1830s, with the reinterment of the prominent lawyer John Philpot Curran and later, the funeral of the cemetery's founder Daniel O'Connell, both of which provided a template for subsequent processions to Glasnevin. From the 1860s onwards these became increasingly politicised nationalist and republican funerals, most famously those of the Home Rule leader Charles Stewart Parnell in 1891 and the veteran Fenian Jeremiah O'Donovan Rossa in 1915. The latter funeral, organised by the IRB, was a major show of strength in the prelude to the Easter Rising, and was the occasion of Patrick Pearse's renowned public utterance: his graveside oration, complete with the famous final line that 'as long as Ireland holds these graves Ireland, unfree, shall never be at peace'.

Such funerals were orchestrated to assert the continuity of the separatist cause and mobilise support for it. All followed a similar pattern: a lying-in-state, followed by a lengthy and invariably well-disciplined procession along a circuitous route. O'Donovan Rossa's grave was beside those of the Fenian leaders James Stephens and John O'Leary, and in 1917 the 1916 veteran Thomas Ashe was buried alongside them. After Ashe's funeral the idea of using this area as a dedicated memorial plot for republicans gathered pace, and the IRB began to buy up graves. The eventual republican plot and its surrounding area is a remarkable who's who of the independence movement and its predecessors.

The firing party, consisting of 8 picked Volunteers, under Captain Liam Clarke, took up a position 10 yards in front of the grave, and fired three volleys over the freshly covered-in grave of their dead comrade. The "Last Post" was sounded by the trumpeters, and Vice-Commandant Michael Collins, standing at the head of the grave, speaking in Irish and then in English, said: "Nothing additional remains to be said. That volley which we have just heard is the only speech which is proper to make above the grave of a dead Fenian."

The Evening Herald *report of 1 October 1917 on the funeral of Thomas Ashe in Glasnevin Cemetery on 30 September 1917.*

Yet there are graves relating to the revolutionary period throughout the cemetery: the dedicated plots to the DMP and RIC, the graves of those killed in the Church Street tenement collapse, the civilian victims of the Rising and Bloody Sunday, and even some of those killed by the IRA on Bloody Sunday can be found throughout the cemetery. The First World War is also represented in Glasnevin. Some of those killed in the sinking of the RMS *Leinster*, torpedoed by a U-boat just outside Dublin Bay in October 1918, are buried here. In recent years the Commonwealth War Graves Commission (CWGC) have marked over 200 graves of Irish soldiers who fought in the British Army in the world wars, the majority of whom fought in the First World War. These men were repatriated and died of injuries and diseases acquired in service; the fact that the graves were not previously marked suggests that many of these came from poorer backgrounds and were unable to afford headstones (the only person interred in Glasnevin to have been killed in combat in the First World War was actually an Irish emigrant who had joined the US Army). The distinctive lozenge-like CWGC markers can be seen throughout the cemetery as well, and Glasnevin also has a 'Cross of Sacrifice', an official CWGC memorial erected in 2014, the first of its kind in the Republic of Ireland. Beside it is the France–Ireland Memorial, unveiled in 2016 and gifted by the French government to recognise the role of Irish solders who fought on French soil in the Franco-Prussian War and the world wars. The cross mounted on it is a replica of a memorial cross erected at Guincy on the Western Front to commemorate the troops of the 16th (Irish) Division; the original is held in the National War Memorial in Islandbridge, though it is not on public display there.

Glasnevin also played a more active role in the revolution. Behind the O'Connell Tower, towards the rear of the cemetery, is the old O'Connell circle, where he was originally interred in 1847 before being moved to his current resting place. One of the vaults was used as an arms dump by the IRA in the War of Independence; guns, ammunition and grenades were hidden in a coffin from which the body had been removed. The dump was never discovered by the British, but when the vault was searched by the National Army during the Civil War, it was empty.

To continue on the route, retrace your steps and go over Cross Guns Bridge, heading towards Phibsborough. Visible on the right will be the floodlights of Dalymount Park.

5 DALYMOUNT PARK

Dalymount Park is at the heart of Phibsborough, and the home of Bohemian Football Club known locally as Bohs. Established in 1890, Bohemians are the longest established association football club in Dublin; the ground that would become Dalymount Park (originally known as 'Pisser Dignam's field') hosted its first match in 1901, and the club eventually enlisted the services of the famous stadium architect Archibald Leitch to design their stadium. Turn into the small laneway off Dalymount Terrace. The football stadium is tucked away behind Victorian red-brick houses. Students of the Hibernian Military School were central to the foundation of the side. While association football has long enjoyed popularity in Dublin, the game (along with cricket and rugby) was denounced by some cultural nationalists (especially within the ranks of the GAA) as essentially unIrish, not least because such games were associated with the British military presence. Yet there were also Irish nationalists who cherished the sport, including former Belfast Celtic goalkeeper and future IRA Dublin Brigade stalwart Oscar Traynor. Equally, Todd Andrews, active in the IRA throughout the War of Independence and Civil War, was another Dublin IRA man who chose association football over the GAA, and who viewed the latter with bemusement as a pastime for countrymen. He would joke of the frustrations of life as an interned prisoner in the Curragh in 1921, as the only code of football the prisoners' leadership allowed was not to his liking.

For Bohemians, the First World War was a defining moment. Harold Sloan, once captain of Bohs and the man who scored the first goal here at Dalymount Park, was killed in action near the Somme in January 1917. British military teams drawn from units stationed in some of the barracks nearby also played in Dalymount; the final of the 'Irish Army Cup' was played here on 22 February 1922, between the Wiltshire Regiment and the Argyll and Sutherland Highlanders, though the match ended 2-2 and went to at least two replays until

the Wiltshires eventually won in Woolwich.

The laneways around Dalymount Park are today home to murals celebrating the place of Bohs in the local community.

■ **WALK 5, STOP 5**

Bohemian F.C. Captain Harold Sloan, killed in the First World War.
(Courtesy Bohemian F.C..)

6 THE PHIBSBOROUGH VOLUNTEER

Continue to the junction at Phibsborough and turn left onto the North Circular Road, walking until you reach Phibsborough Library. Across the road is Leo Broe's impressive monument honouring the local men of the Irish Volunteers and later Irish Republican Army.

Dating from 1939, the monument shows a uniformed Volunteer clutching a rifle, and was unveiled by Dublin Brigade veteran Seán Prendergast. Broe was himself a member of the Irish Volunteers in his youth, and his monument sought to make a connection between the revolutionary period and earlier eras; here, we see depictions around the base of the memorial of events like the death of Brian Boru at the Battle of Clontarf in 1014. The park in which it is located was originally the spur of the Royal Canal that ran west of Mountjoy Prison, the entrance to which is just south of this site on the North Circular Road.

7 SEÁN HEALY PLAQUES

Return to the junction and cross over before turning left; inlaid on the pavement on the south-west corner of the junction is a plaque to Seán Healy, who at the age of fourteen was the youngest rebel to die in the Rising. His family home, further south at 188 Phibsborough Road, is marked by a bronze plaque unveiled during the centenary of the Rising. Healy's father was a member of the Hibernian Rifles, a small nationalist body affiliated to the devoutly Catholic Ancient Order of Hibernians, and Seán Healy himself was a member of Na Fianna Éireann, the republican boy scout group founded by Constance Markievicz and Bulmer Hobson in 1909.

Healy left his home on the morning of 25 April 1916 and made his way to Jacob's factory on Bishop's Street. He was given a message to carry to the Volunteers at Phibsborough by Thomas MacDonagh, who felt him too young to participate in the fighting. Healy was wounded in the head by shrapnel as the British Army fired shells at barricades erected by the insurgents at Phibsborough Corner. He died in the nearby Mater Hospital two days later. A member of the nursing staff in the Mater described his horrific wounds, noting that he arrived in the hospital with 'his brain hanging all over his forehead'.

His family remained committed republicans throughout the revolutionary period, and Healy was widely commemorated by Na Fianna Éireann. He is buried in Glasnevin Cemetery.

8 CONSTITUTION HILL

Continue south along the Phibsborough Road as it becomes Constitution Hill. On the right will be the striking edifice that is Broadstone Station, built in the 1850s as the Dublin depot of the Midlands and Great Western Railway, complete with an impressively colonnaded exterior that covered the train platforms. The main line from Galway terminated here, and was used to bring troops and reinforcements to Dublin during the Easter Rising. Prior to this it had been the venue for a low-key if daring escapade by Seán Heuston and his friend and fellow-volunteer P.J. Stephenson; they went onto the platform as a troop train pulled in and stole a number of rifles.

9 HENRIETTA STREET

The next stop is Henrietta Street, which is approached from here via the imposing facade of the Registry of Deeds. Turn left into King's Inns Park; the opening times may vary throughout the year, so if it is closed, it can be accessed via North King Street, which forms part of the remainder of this route. To the right of the park gate is a London plane tree, dating from the early nineteenth century and called the 'Hungry Tree', because it has engulfed the park bench in front of it. The Registry of Deeds itself was originally built to house the Inns of Court between 1800 and 1817, and was also designed by James Gandon. Perhaps oddly, it is not aligned with Henrietta Street behind it; this was done to maximise the scope for legal chambers and offices, which were to pay off the costs of construction but which were, for the most part, never completed. The triumphal arch behind the building, surmounted with the royal coat of arms, was added in 1820. Pass through the pedestrian gate into Henrietta Street, one of the earliest, most impressive and, sadly, most decayed Georgian streets in Dublin.

In the early eighteenth century a number of major aristocratic, residential districts emerged in Dublin; Henrietta Street was the central focus of one of them. The street lay at the heart of the sprawling estates of the Gardiner family and was supposedly named after one of two Henriettas (either the Duchess of Grafton or the Duchess of Bolton). Of fifteen houses originally built on the street, thirteen remain.

Immediately on the right as you pass through the arch is King's Inns, the central training institution for barristers in Ireland. In June 1920 it was successfully raided by the Dublin IRA, who made off with a substantial cache of weapons. Recounting the raid, Denis Holmes remembered that 'the daring nature of the coup, which was brought off in broad daylight, created a great sensation at the time'. In the raiding party was Kevin Barry, and Holmes recalled him 'coming out of the guardroom with a Lewis gun hugged in his arms'. In total, the IRA took 'about twenty-five rifles, two Lewis guns, a large quantity of ammunition and other military equipment'. Holmes recalled that the King's Inns was viewed as a 'British stronghold' by the IRA, and the raid on it 'created a panic in British military circles'.

> Not far from Broadstone station, in good old Dublin town
> The British troops on sentry stood and nursed their rifles brown
> Then this command "hands up, now stand! If you would save your skins
> For we're here to seize the rifles from the Old King's Inns."

'The Old King's Inns', an anonymous ballad on the IRA raid of June 1920, cited in Terry Moylan, The Indignant Muse: Poetry and Songs of the Irish Revolution, 1887–1926 *(Dublin, 2016).*

Further down the street, on the same side as King's Inns, number 14 now houses the Dublin Tenement Museum. It was one of the last houses on

Henrietta Street, having been developed in the 1740s by Luke Gardiner. It was first occupied by Viscount Molesworth but, like so many houses used or owned by the aristocracy, it became occupied by members of the professional classes after the Act of Union deprived many of the aristocracy of their principal reason for being in Dublin. In the 1850s it was occupied by the Encumbered Estates Court (established to sell off property belonging to wealthy families who had fallen into major debt after the Great Famine) and later by troops from the nearby Linenhall Barracks at the junction of Constitution Hill and North King Street (which was destroyed during the Easter Rising). Ironically, the Encumbered Estates Court sold off much of the Gardiner estate piecemeal, which precipitated its decline into tenements; by 1873 number 14 had become the first building on Henrietta Street to be officially classed as a tenement. During the First World War, a number of its residents enlisted in the British Army, some of whom were killed on the Western Front (as was the case in a number of other houses on the street).

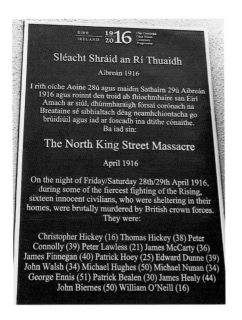

10 NORTH KING STREET

At the bottom of Henrietta Street, turn right onto Bolton Street, which eventually becomes North King Street. On your left, near the junction will Capel Street, is a plaque marking the birthplace of Sean McLoughlin, a young member of the Irish Volunteers whose knowledge of the north inner

■ **WALK 5, STOP 10**
Commemorative plaque to the victims of the North King Street massacre, unveiled during 1916 centenary.

city and bravery saw him given the job of trying to evacuate the GPO garrison from Moore Street; he was promoted in the process. McLoughlin maintained, credibly, that James Connolly had appointed him to his own rank of Commandant-General after Connolly had been incapacitated by his wounds. While the precise rank was disputed, what is not in dispute is that McLoughlin took charge of the final surrender of the GPO garrison. He remained active in the revolution thereafter as an IRA organiser in Munster, was involved in founding the Communist Party of Ireland and fought in Limerick and Tipperary during the Civil War, in which he took the anti-Treaty side, hoping that the IRA could become a vehicle for class politics. Having been imprisoned by the Free State in December 1922, McLoughlin became an active trade unionist after his release from captivity, and as a senior member of the Larkinite Workers' Union of Ireland oversaw a strike in 1924 aimed at improving pay and conditions for workers at the Great Southern and Western Railway's Inchicore rail works. His role here brought him into acrimonious conflict with Jim Larkin, who came to an agreement with the railway, thereby undermining McLoughlin (and sacrificing the jobs of 107 members of his own union). A disillusioned McLoughlin emigrated to England soon after, eventually settling in Sheffield, where he died in 1960.

Continue walking west along Bolton Street and North King Street. The area directly behind the Four Courts, extending up Church Street towards Phibsborough, was, after the GPO, the main area of insurgent activity north of the River Liffey during the Easter Rising. This area included North King Street and the Linenhall Barracks (which was burned down, though a fragment of a wall remains at the southern edge of the park beside King's Inns). Its location gave it a strategic importance. It was adjacent to the north quays, which ensured that Volunteers in this area were in a position to interfere with troop movements to and from both the Royal Barracks and Kingsbridge (Heuston) Station, the terminus of the Great Southern and Western Railway. North of the area seized by the Volunteers was Broadstone Station, the terminus of the Midland Great Western Railway, which was another venue that could facilitate the arrival of reinforcements into the city. In line with the manner in which fighting intensified as the week wore on, the area around Church Street, Brunswick Street and North King Street saw some of the heaviest and most intense fighting in the city during the Rising, though much of North King Street has been redeveloped and bears little resemblance to its original form.

North King Street also saw the worst atrocities against civilians to take place during the Rising. As the week wore on, the South Staffordshire regiment made its way through the streets here with great difficulty, advancing a mere 150 yards over two days, and losing fourteen men in the process. On 28–29 April 1916 soldiers made their way into a number of homes in the area. At 170 North King Street, three men were killed and their bayoneted remains were discovered buried in the back garden. Similarly, two men were killed in numbers 172 and 174 respectively, while four bodies were found in the basement of 27. These were just some of the killings on the street, attributed to the anger and frustration of the soldiers at their slow progress here. General Sir John Maxwell, the British military governor, sought to excuse the killings on the grounds that the civilians in the district had been sympathisers with the rebels, but news of the deaths on North King Street outraged public opinion, with Dublin Corporation demanding an inquiry into events; it was also denounced in Westminster by IPP MPs. The deaths here, along with the killing of Francis Sheehy-Skeffington at Portobello Barracks, played no small part in shaping public opinion after the Rising, not least when the inquiry into the events on North King Street found no soldiers guilty of any wrongdoing.

Continue along North King Street until you reach the junction with Church Street and Constitution Hill. The area has been heavily redeveloped. Patrick Monk's bakery on 79–80 Upper Church Street was located near the junction, and this is where the eighteen-year-old IRA volunteer Kevin Barry was captured in 1920. Barry was the son of a dairyman and was a student in University College Dublin when, on 20 September 1920, he and a number of others ambushed a group of British soldiers collecting bread at the bakery in order to steal their weapons (some weeks previously Barry had been involved in the successful raid for weapons on the nearby King's Inns). Shots were exchanged; one solder was killed and two were fatally wounded, while Barry was captured as he hid beneath a lorry. He was the first member of the IRA to be captured carrying out an attack since the Easter Rising of 1916; despite his youth, on 20 October 1920 he became the first to be executed under new and draconian laws directed against the IRA. His death at such a young age, despite a campaign for clemency, made him one of the most famous republican martyrs of the war, and he was the subject of one of the best-known ballads of the period,

■ **WALK 5**

A contemporary US newspaper comments on the failure of the rebellion. Notice the rebellion was 'Made in Germany'. (Library of Congress)

which would later be sung by performers as diverse as Paul Robeson and Leonard Cohen.

Also at the junction with North King Street, beside the Constitution Hill social housing scheme, is a plaque commemorating the fifteen civilian men and boys killed here towards the end of the Easter Rising.

11 CHURCH STREET

At the junction, turn left onto Church Street; an area with multiple associations with the revolutionary period. The memorial park on the left of the street marks the deaths of six people killed when two tenement houses, at 66–67 Church Street, collapsed on 2 September 1913. This happened just after the beginning of the 1913 Lockout (indeed, one of those killed was on strike at the time), and led to a public inquiry into the condition of the slums. The lockout was not automatically linked to the poverty of Dublin's slums, but given that Jim Larkin's ITGWU sought to organise unskilled labour, the vast majority of whom lived in the slums, it was inevitable that it was in Dublin's tenements that the impact of the lockout was most keenly felt. Infant mortality rates rose through the winter of 1913–14 as homes were deprived of an income. One of those killed in the collapse, Eugene Salmon, had been locked out of employment only a day earlier.

The inquiry that followed the Church Street disaster estimated that the number of tenements in Dublin had increased from 353 to 1,682 during the Great Famine, thence to 5,995 in 1850, 'some of which are still in use as tenement houses'. By 1880 there were 9,760. The 1913 inquiry painted a horrific picture of tenement life: 73,973 people, including families, lived in single-room dwellings and 22,701 individuals lived in dwellings that were officially deemed unfit for human habitation. The inquiry's generalised description of a Dublin tenement could have been culled from any number of official reports of informal accounts of Dublin's slums in the nineteenth century: 'the tenement houses of the present day are for the most part houses that were originally built to accommodate and provide for one family, and as a rule they face a thoroughfare of the city, though some are to be found in courts and alleys. The tenement houses as a whole are exceedingly old structures, and are more or less in an advanced state of decay'. They were usually served by a single tap for water and a single toilet; it seems that these were rarely used by women, and there were no special facilities for children. Houses were filthy, with human excrement commonly scattered around, though some were kept tidy and decorated at Christmas; there was no privacy, and landlords were reluctant to rent to young families. Tenement life was 'physically and morally bad', and the report recommended that it should be eradicated; after all, 'some of these structures scarcely deserve the name of house'.

While the inquiry that followed the Church Street disaster went some way to revealing the shocking extent of the problem, moves towards tackling the issue were derailed by the outbreak of the First World War.

The red-brick houses on the street were built to replace the slums here, and date from 1917. Directly across the road is Father Mathew Hall, which was used as Edward Daly's headquarters during the Easter Rising. The Capuchin Friars based on Church Street, such as Fathers Albert Bibby and Augustine Hayden, ministered to the 1916 leaders before their executions, and continued to play a similar role at intervals throughout the revolution.

The first thing that came to my notice, on proceeding on the inspection, was a mob of some hundreds of people attempting to force their way into Monks Bakery Shop, North King Street, for the purpose of getting bread. I obtained two Volunteers with rifles, whom I placed inside the door of the shop and, in the hearing of the mob, gave them orders to shoot any person attempting to enter. I then told the mob that any able-bodied men amongst them, who would come and assist me by carrying some materials for me, would receive bread. A considerable number came to assist me. These people were used for the purpose of carrying building materials from the site of houses being built in Church Street, opposite the Father Mathew Hall. All this material was used to strengthen the barricades in the vicinity.

Liam O'Carroll of the Irish Volunteers recalls an incident on Church Street during the Easter Rising; the rubble he refers to may well have been from the site of the houses being reconstructed after the tenement collapse of 1913. Military Archives BMH WS 314.

12 THE FOUR COURTS

Continue south along Church Street, and you will come to the vast complex of the Four Courts, originally built between 1776 and 1802, to a design by Thomas Cooley and James Gandon. It is, along with the Custom House, one of the two most substantial Georgian buildings north of the Liffey, and was built to house the main system of courts, because in the seventeenth and eighteenth centuries, the legal profession had become clustered in and around this area and Christ Church. It was deliberately built to dominate, facing onto the river, and topped with a dome (modelled on St Paul's Cathedral in London and the Pantheon in Rome) that compensated for the fact that it was built on a bend in the river that obscured the views of the building from the east. The sculptures on the pediment represent Moses, Justice and Mercy; those on the parapet represent Authority and Wisdom. The decorative motifs are made of Portland stone, while the main structure is composed of granite. It is also quite battle-scarred. The building was the venue for fighting during the 1916 Rising but the most notable damage came during the Civil War.

In April 1922 the Four Courts had been occupied and fortified by the anti-Treaty IRA under Rory O'Connor; and the Civil War would begin with an attack on the building by the new National Army of the Irish Free State on 28 June 1922, after the British had lost patience with what they viewed as the tardiness of the Provisional Government in dealing with the anti-Treaty IRA; the assassination of Sir Henry Wilson in London, shot dead on his doorstep by two members of the IRA, was the last straw. The British were prepared to act themselves, but decided to give Michael Collins an ultimatum instead. The Four Courts was surrounded, with National Army troops taking up positions around the perimeter of the complex, including the Medical Mission on Chancery Place, the tower of St Michan's Church on Church Street and the Jameson Distillery on Smithfield. The real damage, however, came from 18 lb field guns borrowed from the British and deployed south of the Liffey at the foot of Bridgefoot Street and Lower Bridge Street. The inexperienced gunners under Emmet Dalton initially had only shrapnel shells, which did little damage to the stonework. They were soon supplied with explosive shells, which did more substantial damage. The defenders seem to have had plans to burn the

DESTRUCTION OF FOUR COURTS

WITH ALL ITS HISTORIC DOCUMENTS THROUGH FIRE CAUSED BY

IRREGULARS' EXPLOSION OF MINE

The following was issued by G.H.Q., Irish Army, on the 4th July :—

A CONNECTED MINE.

Those who were in the Hall of the Four Courts at the time of the Explosion are well aware that it was a Mine Exploded, *and that it was Connected.* Other Connected Mines have since been removed from the Four Courts. Our Men were in the Hall when the Explosion took place. At that time the Fire had not reached that part of the Building.

NO SHELL.

No Shell came near that part of the Building while our Men were there.

OTHER TRAPS TO KILL.

Other Traps were laid with the intention of Slaughtering our Troops *after their occupation of the Building,* but this was the only one that Succeeded. One of these Traps was a Mine concealed by a Typewriter Cover. In a letter dated, June 29, addressed, "O.C. 5.," Mr. Oscar Traynor, a Leader of the Irregulars wrote : "Congratulations on your Mine. If you have no more of these let me know."

One of the Irregulars' Leaders, Mr. Ernest O'Malley assured Brigadier-Gen. O'Daly " That the Mine was Exploded by the Irregulars in the Four Courts". HE ALSO EXPRESSED REGRET THAT THE CASUALTIES AMONG THE TROOPS WERE NOT GREATER.

WALK 5, STOP 12 ■

Handbill issued by Free State forces following the destruction of Public Records Office, 1922. (Wikimedia Commons)

building and retreat; they had also used the Public Record Office (PRO) in the complex as a munitions dump. On 30 June two huge explosions preceded the surrender of the IRA garrison in the Four Courts as the arms dumps detonated; the precise cause remains unclear, but it was probably caused by fires in the complex reaching the explosives that were being stored. The scale of the devastation can be seen on the west side of the Four Courts, as you continue up Church Street; the western wall is pockmarked by small-arms fire, while the newer office block inside the complex marks where the original was destroyed. In the process, a vast quantity of historical documents held in the PRO were also destroyed, an irretrievable loss that ensures huge swathes of the Irish past can never be explored.

> *The yard was littered with chunks of masonry and smouldering records; pieces of white paper were yet gyrating in the upper air like seagulls. The explosion seemed to give an extra push to roaring orange flames which formed patterns across the sky. Fire was fascinating to watch; it had a spell like running water. Flame sang and conducted its own orchestra simultaneously. It can't be long now, I though, until the real noise comes. The dome had been lifted by the shock.*

Ernie O'Malley describes the destruction of the Four Courts from inside the building, in his memoir The Singing Flame *(Cork, 1978).*

With that, we have almost come full circle. Once you have reached the quays, walk west along the north quays, away from the city, until you come to Collins Barracks, where the first walk began. Or, to learn more about what has been described in this book, just keep reading.

DRAMATIS PERSONAE

This list is by no means a complete overview of all who participated in or actively opposed the Irish revolution in Dublin. Rather, it is intended to provide a brief overview of some of the recurring figures who appear throughout this book.

Ashe, Thomas (1885–1917). Born in Kerry, Ashe worked as a school principal in Corduff, north County Dublin. Active in the Gaelic League and the IRB. Successfully commanded the Irish Volunteers at Ashbourne in 1916. First president of the IRB post-1916, Ashe died on hunger strike in Mountjoy Prison in September 1917.

Barry, Kevin (1902–1918). Born at Fleet Street in Dublin, Barry joined the IRA in 1917 at the age of fifteen. Hanged in 1920 for his involvement in an IRA ambush in Dublin's north inner city. He became the first republican executed since the Easter Rising.

Barry, Tom (1897–1980). Kerry-born republican, though synonymous with Cork for his leadership of Third West Cork Flying Column during War of Independence. He had served in the British Army during the First World War. An opponent of the Treaty, he remained active within the IRA in the 1930s. Author of *Guerrilla Days in Ireland*, an influential memoir of the War of Independence.

Broy, Eamon (1887–1972). Born in Kildare. Worked within the Dublin Metropolitan Police intelligence division ('G Division') during War of Independence. Provided information to republicans. Smuggled Michael Collins into G Division headquarters in April 1919. Supported Anglo-Irish Treaty. Later commissioner of the Gardaí, whose Special Branch became known as 'Broy Harriers'.

Brugha, Cathal (1874–1922). Born Charles Burgess in Dublin. A leading member of the Irish Volunteers from the time of the inception of the body. Second in command at South Dublin Union during Rising. Served on IRA General Headquarters staff during War of Independence. Opposed Treaty, killed in action in Dublin in 1922.

Carson, Edward (1854–1932). Born on Harcourt Street in Dublin's south inner city. Educated at Trinity College Dublin. A barrister by trade who famously prosecuted Oscar Wilde, he entered politics in 1892 elected as a Unionist MP representing Trinity College Dublin. Leader of opposition to Home Rule, considered a founding father of Northern Ireland, despite his own opposition to partition. A statue in his honour stands outside the Stormont parliament building in Belfast.

Casement, Roger (1864–1916). Born in Dublin into an Anglo-Irish household, Casement came to international prominence as a British civil servant and humanitarian activist, exposing human rights abuses in the Congo. Rejecting imperialism, he became active in Irish separatism. Central to establishing contact with Germany before Easter Rising, captured at Banna Strand near Kerry and hanged for treason in August 1916.

Ceannt, Éamonn (1881–1916). Born in Galway, Ceannt was active in cultural nationalist politics, including the Gaelic League. A member of Sinn Féin, he was sworn into the Fenians in 1912 by Seán Mac Diarmada. Signatory of the 1916 Proclamation.

Clarke, Thomas Thomas (1858–1916). Born at Hurst Castle in England, the son of a British Army sergeant. Joined the IRB at a young age, participated in the ill-fated Fenian dynamite campaign of the 1880s. Served fifteen years in Pentonville and other British prisons. Signatory of 1916 proclamation and arguably its key leader.

Collins, Michael (1890–1922). Born in County Cork. Sworn into the Irish Republican Brotherhood by Sam Maguire in London.

Aide-de-camp to Joseph Plunkett during Easter Rising, he rose to prominence in its aftermath. IRA Director of Intelligence during War of Independence. President of IRB from 1920 until his death. Chairman of the Provisional Government in 1922. Killed in an ambush in Cork in August 1922.

Connolly, James (1868–1916). Edinburgh-born Marxist and trade union organiser. Active with the Industrial Workers' of the World in America and the ITGWU and Irish Citizen Army in Dublin. Editor of *The Workers' Republic*. Signatory of 1916 Proclamation.

Cosgrave, William Thomas (1880–1965). Born in Dublin. Sinn Féin councillor on Dublin Corporation from 1909 until 1920. Veteran of the Easter Rising, elected MP for Kilkenny in the 1918 election. A supporter of the Anglo-Irish Treaty, Cosgrave was the first elected head of government in the Irish Free State.

Daly, Edward (1891–1916). Born in Limerick, Daly came from a staunchly Fenian family. Commandant of the First Battalion of the Irish Volunteers in Dublin, he led the occupation of the Four Courts during the Easter Rising. Youngest of the executed 1916 leaders.

De Valera, Éamon (1882–1975). Born in New York City, educated in Limerick and Dublin. Commander at Boland's Mills during Easter Rising. Elected head of both Sinn Féin and the Irish Volunteers post-1916, President of Dáil Éireann during revolutionary period. Opponent of Anglo-Irish Treaty and founder of Fianna Fáil. Later Taoiseach and President.

Griffith, Arthur (1871–1922). Born in Dublin. A nationalist journalist and editor, he co-founded the U*nited Irishman* newspaper in 1899. Founder of Sinn Féin party in 1905. Leader of Irish delegation in Treaty debates, Griffith supported the Anglo-Irish Treaty. Died of a brain haemorrhage in August 1922.

Hackett, Rosie (1892–1976). Born in Dublin. Joined the ITGWU while employed by Jacob's factory. Later a founding member of the Irish Women's Workers' Union. Member of St Stephen's Green garrison at Easter Week. Active in labour politics generally in subsequent decades.

Heuston, Seán (1891–1916). Born in Dublin, railway clerk and a prominent leader within the Na Fianna Éireann, the nationalist boy scout movement. Officer commanding the Irish Volunteers at the Mendicity Institution. Executed for his role in the Rising.

Hobson, Bulmer (1883–1969). Born into a Belfast Quaker family, Hobson was influential in reviving the IRB in the early twentieth century. Co-founder of Na Fianna Éireann, founding member of Irish Volunteers. Opposed to insurrection in 1916, he was kidnapped on the eve of the Rising to prevent interference in plans. Subsequently played no role in independence movement.

Larkin, James (1876–1947). Liverpool-born trade union organiser. Founder of ITGWU and the Labour Party. Imprisoned in United States from 1920–1923; a divisive figure who remained involved in labour politics until his death.

MacBride, John (1868–1916). Born in Westport into a family with strong Fenian connections, MacBride achieved renown as a leader in the Irish Brigade which participated in the Second Boer War (1899–1902) on the side of the Boers. Second in command to Thomas MacDonagh at Jacob's factory during Easter Rising. Executed for his role in the Rising.

Mac Diarmada, Seán [John MacDermott] (1883–1916). Raised in Leitrim, Mac Diarmada was active in the Gaelic League and the Ancient Order of Hibernians in his youth. Later an organiser for the Sinn Féin party, as an active IRB he edited *Irish Freedom*, the newspaper of the movement from 1910. Signatory of the 1916 proclamation. Executed for his role in the Rising.

MacDonagh, Thomas (1878–1916). Born in Tipperary, MacDonagh was a revolutionary separatist, poet and educationalist. A teacher at St Enda's, he also lectured at the National University. A founding member of the ASTI trade union. Commanded the rebel forces at Jacob's factory. A signatory of the 1916 proclamation. Executed for his role in the Rising.

McKee, Dick (1893–1920). Born in Dublin. Participated in Easter Rising, coming to prominence as an IRA leader in War of Independence. Director of Training for IRA, instrumental to establishing 'The Squad' on the orders of Michael Collins. Killed on Bloody Sunday 1920 while in British custody.

MacNeill, Eoin (1867–1945). Born in County Antrim. A founding member of the Gaelic League and a distinguished academic historian. First Professor of Early and Medieval Irish History at University College Dublin. Chief of Staff of the Irish Volunteers, though not privy to plans for insurrection. Supported Anglo-Irish Treaty and appointed Minister for Education in 1922.

Markievicz, Constance (1868–1927). London-born revolutionary nationalist, socialist and suffrage campaigner. Born into the aristocratic Anglo-Irish Gore-Booth family of Sligo, she married a Polish count, Casimir Markievicz, and was usually known as Countess Markievicz. Co-founder of Na Fianna Éireann boy scouts and active within the Irish Citizen Army and Cumann na mBan. Sentenced to execution for her role in the Rising, her sentence was commuted. First female MP elected to Westminster parliament. Minister for Labour in Dáil government

■ *The bronze bust of Constance Markievicz, by sculptor Seamus Murphy, in St Stephen's Green.*

Mellows, Liam (1892–1922). Born in Lancashire, Mellows joined Na Fianna Éireann at a young age. A founding member of the Irish Volunteers, Mellows led the Easter Rising in Galway. Elected a Sinn Féin MP in the 1918 election, he rejected the Anglo-Irish Treaty and was among the IRA men to seize the Four Courts. Executed on 8 December 1922.

Molony, Helena (1883–1967). Born in Dublin. Active with Inghinidhe na hÉireann and later the Irish Citizen Army. An actor with the Abbey Theatre. A committed trade unionist, she served as president of the Irish Trade Union Congress post-independence.

Neligan, David (1899–1983). Born in Limerick. Joined the DMP in 1917, recruited into G Division in 1919. Known as 'The Spy in the Castle' for his services to Michael Collins. Supported Anglo-Irish Treaty. Participated in seaborne attacks on republican positions in Munster during Civil War.

O'Donnell, Peadar (1893–1986). Born in Donegal. An active trade union organiser with the ITGWU from 1918. Active in the IRA during War of Independence, he opposed the Treaty and was among the IRA men to occupy Four Courts. A leading socialist activist over decades and co-founder of *The Bell* journal in 1946.

O'Malley, Ernie (1897–1957). Born in Mayo and raised in Dublin. A medical student at the time of the Easter Rising, he joined the Volunteers in its aftermath. A national organiser for the IRA during War of Independence, he opposed the Anglo-Irish Treaty. Later a writer and distinguished literary figure.

Pearse, Patrick (1879–1916). Born at Great Brunswick Street in Dublin, the son of sculptor James Pearse. A teacher and poet, he was principal of St Enda's, an innovative bilingual school at The Hermitage in Rathfarnham. Signatory of the 1916 proclamation and 'President of the Provisional Government'. Executed for his role in the Rising.

Pearse, William (1881–1916). Younger brother of Patrick. A graduate of the Metropolitan School of Art, he followed his father as a sculptor. Later a teacher at St Enda's. Executed for his involvement in the Rising.

Plunkett, Joseph Mary (1887–1916). Born at Upper Fitzwilliam Street in Dublin, Plunkett joined the IRB in 1915 and travelled to Germany seeking military assistance for insurrection. A poet and cultural nationalist, he participated in the Easter Rising despite ill-health. Signatory of the 1916 Proclamation. Executed for his role in the Rising.

Redmond, John Edward (1856–1918). Born in Wexford, Redmond served as leader of the Irish Parliamentary Party from 1900 until 1918. As a constitutional nationalist MP he championed the cause of Home Rule for Ireland. Supported British war effort on outbreak of First World War.

Sheehy-Skeffington, Francis (1878–1916). Born Francis Skeffington in Cavan. A contemporary and friend of James Joyce at University College Dublin. Editor of Irish suffrage newspaper *The Irish Citizen* and an activist with the Irish Women's Franchise League, which he co-founded. Murdered during the Easter Rising at Portobello Barracks, despite his non-participation.

Sheehy-Skeffington, Hanna (1877–1946). Born Hanna Sheehy in Cork. Founder of the Irish Women's Franchise League. Prominent anti-war campaigner following the outbreak of First World War. Opponent of the Anglo-Irish Treaty and a committed republican and feminist campaigner post-independence, assistant editor of *An Phoblacht* for a period in the 1930s.

Traynor, Oscar (1886–1963). Born in Dublin, Traynor was a noted footballer in his youth. Goalkeeper to Belfast Celtic Football Club from 1910 to 1912. Brigadier to the Dublin Brigade of the IRA during War of Independence. Opposed Anglo-Irish Treaty and commanded republican forces on O'Connell Street during Battle of Dublin. Later a founding member of Fianna Fáil and Minister for Defence.

Wyse Power, Jennie (1858–1941). Born in Wicklow. Veteran Ladies' Land League campaigner and founder of Sinn Féin and Inghinidhe na hÉireann. The 1916 proclamation was signed at her business premises, the Irish Farm Produce Company on Henry Street. A supporter of the Anglo-Irish Treaty. Member of Seanad Éireann.

Yeats, William Butler (1865–1939). Born in Dublin. Educated between London and Dublin. Greatly influenced by Fenian radical John O'Leary. Distinguished poet and co-founder of Dublin's Abbey Theatre in 1904. Senator in Irish Free State parliament. Winner of the Nobel Prize for Literature, 1924.

VISITOR ATTRACTIONS ALONG THE ROUTES

Many of the sites that you will come across are public, some (such as the barracks) remain private, but many are also visitor attractions; conditions of access can vary, and we have listed them below, should you wish to check before a possible visit.

Abbey Theatre: www.abbeytheatre.ie
Custom House: www.housing.gov.ie/corporate/1916-2016-centenary-programme/custom-house-visitor-centre
Dublin Castle: www.dublincastle.ie
Dublin City Hall: www.dublincity.ie/dublincityhall
Croke Park: crokepark.ie
Glasvenin Cemetery Museum: www.glasnevinmuseum.ie
GPO: www.gpowitnesshistory.ie
Guinness Storehouse: www.guinness-storehouse.com/en
Kilmainham Gaol Museum: www.kilmainhamgaolmuseum.ie
Phoenix Park: www.phoenixpark.ie
Richmond Barracks: www.richmondbarracks.ie
Royal Hospital Kilmainham/IMMA: www.heritageireland.ie/en/dublin/royalhospitalkilmainham/
Marsh's Library: www.marshlibrary.ie
National Museum of Ireland (Decorative Arts and History), Collins Barracks: www.museum.ie/Decorative-Arts-History
OPW sites: Arbour Hill, the Garden of Remembrance, Irish National
War Memorial Gardens: opwdublincommemorative.ie
St Stephen's Green: www.ststephensgreenpark.ie

ONLINE RESOURCES

There are a number of reference works and online resources that contain a great deal of material on Dublin in the revolutionary period: the *Dictionary of Irish Biography* (7 vols, Cambridge, 2009) is particularly useful, as are the major Dublin newspapers (such as *The Irish Times*, *Irish Independent*, and *The Freeman's Journal*). Many of these can be accessed via the Irish Newspaper Archive (www.irishnewsarchive.com); likewise, a wide range of periodical material is available via the JSTOR database (www.jstor.org). There are a number of extremely useful online resources which we have used extensively, most especially the Bureau of Military History, which we have made extensive use of (www.bureauofmilitaryhistory.ie/), the Irish Military Archives (www.militaryarchives.ie/home), and the *Century Ireland* project: www.rte.ie/centuryireland/. Other online resources for the revolutionary period are listed on the official Decade of Centenaries website: www.decadeofcentenaries.com/. Other websites of more general interest are: Archiseek: archiseek.com; Come here to me!: comeheretome.com; Dublin City Architects: www.dublincityarchitects.ie; Dublin ghost signs: dublinghostsigns.com; 1901 & 1911 census: www.census.nationalarchives.ie; Dublin City Public Libraries Heritage and History: www.dublincity.ie/main-menu-services-recreation-culture-dublin-city-public-libraries-and-archive/heritage-and-history.

SELECT BIBLIOGRAPHY

Barry, Michael, *Victorian Dublin Revealed* (Dublin, 2011).

Carey, Tim, *Dublin Since 1922* (Dublin, 2016).

Casey, Christine, *Dublin: the City between the Grand and Royal Canals* (New Haven, 2005).

Connell, Joseph E.A., *Dublin Rising 1916* (Dublin, 2015)

— *Michael Collins' Dublin, 1916–22* (Dublin, 2017)

Corlett, Christiaan, Darkest Dublin: *The Story of the Church Street Disaster and a Pictorial Account of the Slums of Dublin in 1913* (Dublin, 2008).

Crowe, Catriona, *Dublin 1911* (Dublin, 2011).

Crowley, John, Donal Ó Drisceoil and Mike Murphy (eds), John Borgonovo (associate ed.), *Atlas of the Irish Revolution* (Cork, 2017).

Daly, Mary E., Dublin: *The Deposed Capital: A Social and Economic*

History, 1860–1914 (Cork, 1984).

Devine, Francis (ed.) *A Capital in Conflict: Dublin City and the 1913 Lockout* (Dublin 2013).

Dickson, David, *Dublin: The Making of a Capital* (London, 2014).

Dorney, John, *Griffith College: A History of the Campus, 1813–2013* (Dublin, 2013)

— *The Civil War in Dublin: The Fight For The Irish Capital, 1922–24* (Dublin, 2017).

Dougan, Quincy, 'Dublin's loyal volunteers', *History Ireland 22.3* (May/June 2014).

Durney, James, 'How Aungier Street/Camden Street became known as 'the Dardanelles', *The Irish Sword, 27: 108* (2010).

Fagan, Terry, *Monto: Murders, Madams and Black Coddle* (Dublin, 2000).

Fallon, Donal, *The Pillar: The Life and Afterlife of the Nelson Pillar* (Dublin, 2014).

Fallon, Las, *Dublin Fire Brigade and the Irish Revolution* (Dublin, 2012).

Foster, R.F., *Vivid Faces: The Revolutionary Generation in Ireland, 1890–1923* (London, 2014).

Gibney, John, *A History of the Easter Rising in 50 Objects* (Cork, 2016).

Gibney, John (ed.), *Dublin City Council and the 1916 Rising* (Dublin, 2016).

Gillis, Liz, *The Fall of Dublin* (Cork, 2011).

Gillis Liz & McAuliffe, Mary, *Richmond Barracks 1916: We Were There: 77 Women of the Easter Rising* (Dublin, 2016)

Irish, Tomás, *Trinity in War and Revolution, 1912–23* (Dublin, 2015)

Kevin C. Kearns, *Dublin Tenement Life* (Dublin, 1996)

McGarry, Fearghal, *The Rising Ireland: Easter 1916* (Oxford, 2010).

McGarry, Fearghal, *The Abbey Rebels: A Lost Revolution* (Dublin, 2015).

McElligott, Jason, 'In the line of fire', *History Ireland, 20.3* (May/June 2012).

Ó Conchubair, Brian (ed.), *Dublin's Fighting Story, 1916–21: Told by the Men Who Made It* (2nd ed. Cork, 2009).

Gearóid Ó Tuathaigh (ed.), *The GAA and Revolution in Ireland, 1913–1923* (Cork, 2015)

Prunty, Jacinta, *Managing the Dublin Slums, 1850–1922* (Dublin, 2004).

Rains, Stephanie, *Commodity Culture and Social Class in Dublin, 1850–1916* (Dublin, 2010).

Rigney, Peter, 'Easter Week 1916 and the Great Southern & Western Railway', *Journal of the Irish Railway Record Society, 22: 160* (2006).

Rowley, Ellen (ed.), *More Than Concrete Blocks: Dublin City's Twentieth-Century Buildings and their Stories, vol 1: 1900–40* (Dublin, 2016).

Sheehan, William, *Fighting for Dublin: the British Battle for Dublin, 1919–21* (Cork, 2007).

Whelan, Yvonne, *Reinventing Dublin: Streetscape, Iconography and the Politics of Identity* (Dublin 2003).

Yeates, Padraig, *Lockout: Dublin 1913* (2001).

— *A City in Wartime: Dublin, 1914–18* (Dublin, 2011).

— *A City in Turmoil: Dublin, 1919–21* (Dublin, 2013).

— *A City in Civil War: Dublin, 1921–23* (Dublin, 2015).

— *Rioters, Looters, Lady Patrols & Mutineers: Some Reflections on Lesser Visited Aspects of the Irish Revolution in Dublin* (Dublin, 2017).

INDEX

FIRST PUBLISHED IN 2018 BY
The Collins Press
West Link Park
Doughcloyne
Wilton
Cork
T12 N5EF
Ireland

A CIP record for this book is available from the British Library.

Paperback ISBN: 978-1-84889-339-9

Design and typesetting by Gigantic Media
Typeset in Bebas Neue & OpenSans
Printed in Poland by Białostockie Zakłady Graficzne SA